Red Sulphur Springs, West Virginia

A Nineteenth Century Health Spa
in the Allegheny Foreland

by Fred Ziegler

35th Star Publishing
Charleston, West Virginia
www.35thstar.com

Copyright. © 2024 by Fred Ziegler.
All Rights Reserved.
First edition, 2024.
Printed in the United States of America.

No part of this publication may be reproduced, distributed or transmitted in any form or by any means, including photocopying, recording, or other electronic or mechanical methods, without the prior written permission of the publisher, except in the case of brief quotations embodied in critical reviews and certain other noncommercial uses permitted by copyright law.

ISBN-13: 979-8-9889020-4-1
Library of Congress Control Number: 2024935711

35th Star Publishing
Charleston, West Virginia
www.35thstar.com

Cover design by Studio 6 Sense
Interior design by 35th Star Publishing

On the cover:
Photograph of pavilion at Red Sulphur Springs, Trixie Martin collection.
Painting of Red Sulphur Springs by Edward Beyer, orginally published in his portfolio, *Album of Virginia*.
Newspaper advertisement for Red Sulphur Springs, *The Charleston Mercury*, Charleston, South Carolina,
   June 25, 1856, page 3.

Table of Contents

Acknowledgments	vii
Introduction	1
1 - Nicholas Harvey and the Early Days of the Springs, 1795-1826	5
2 - James Harvey, the Pavilion, and Some Early Visitor Records, 1826-1832	13
3 - William Burke, Builder and Promoter, 1832-1842	21
4 - Transportation in the Mid-Nineteenth Century	31
5 - The Owner Families: Beirne, Dunlap, and Campbell, 1843-1861	43
6 - The Civil War Years and the Fate of the Local Resorts	53
7 - The Dunlap, Campbell, and Adair Owners and the Reconstruction Years, 1865-1879	59
8 - Levi P. Morton, New York Friends, and an Era of Absentee Ownership, 1880-1896	69
9 - Levi P. Morton and the Final Years of Red Sulphur Springs, 1896-1927	77
10 - Earth Science and the Origin of the Minerals in the Springs	85
Appendices	
One - External Influences on the Economy of the West Virginia Resorts	93
Two - Excerpts from Yellow Fever Articles from 1820 to 1830	95
Three - Medicinal Effects of Local Mineral Springs as Summarized in 1835	97
Four - An 1846 Classification of Mineral Water Types	99
Five - Red Sulphur Springs District: Interesting History in the Long Ago, 1847-1930	101
Six - A Deed from the Monroe County Courthouse	105
Seven - Red Sulphur Owner Wm. Noble Remarries His Wife After Obtaining a Divorce	109
Bibliography	111
Index	117
About the Author	121

Acknowledgments

Vernessa Pontius, for cataloging our museum literature and searching out several obscure references on Red Sulphur Springs.

Jimmy Costa, life-long collector for providing an 1827-29 Day Book of Red Sulphur visitors.

Trixie Martin, for making available for use, her large collection of photographs and paintings.

David Ziegler, lawyer for reviewing the numerous legal records for The Red and helping to interpret them.

Judy Azulay and Toni Ogden for help and advice in sorting and managing the computer files.

Judy Wagner for doing a very thorough job on copy-editing the manuscript.

Ba Rea for preparing the map of the region.

Introduction

"The region of the Virginia Springs straddled the continental divide, sprawling through the long valleys and over the equally long ridges of the Alleghenies. Anyone beginning at the Warm Springs, which was the northwesterly point of the region, and drawing a line around the principal watering places would have traced a lop-sided, diamond-shaped kite pointing northeast and southwest, with Warm Springs at the top and Gray Sulphur Springs at the bottom. The central axis running between them would be about seventy-five miles long and the transverse axis, running cross country from east to west between Rockbridge Alum in the east and Blue Sulphur on the west, would be approximately the same. Down through the center lay the inner group, the fountains most strongly impregnated with minerals, heat, fashion, and fame—the Warm, the Hot, the White Sulphur, the Sweet, the Salt and the Red Sulphur" (Perceval Reniers, 1941, *The Springs of Virginia; Life, Love, and Death at the Waters—1775-1900*, pp.25-6).

Thus, the Red Sulphur Springs resort was a member of a large and exclusive array of mineral spas and, like the best, enjoyed a popularity throughout the nineteenth century and beyond. However, this long history has never been adequately summarized, and the purpose of this book is to address this oversight as well as to tell an interesting story. See Table 0.1 for a list of the primary information sources used in preparing this book. This Introduction covers the diversity of topics to be addressed.

The ownership and owners' lives will be reconstructed for each of the individuals or partners because this is the most straightforward means of establishing a temporal framework for this history. Pioneer Nicholas Harvey and sons James and John were first to develop a primitive health spa about 1795 consisting of log houses and accommodating about 40 visitors. Polymath William Burke was next in 1832 and invested heavily in the famous "cottage rows" but eventually went bankrupt and then proved his real skill in writing books about the experience. The local Beirne and Dunlap families then bought into the resort in 1845 and were joined by the Campbell family in about 1858. These three families continued through the Civil War and beyond until only their descendants were left to run it. Finally, wealthy politician Levi P. Morton acquired the resort in 1880 and invested money in upgrading the facilities but he became Vice President of the United States in 1889 and then Governor of New York from 1895-96. During this "inter-regnum" Red Sulphur was managed by a series of New York businessmen including friends and relatives of Morton. Eventually, Morton reacquired it in 1896 and eventually sold it in 1917 to a local group headed by banker E.C. Hansbarger. This group ran the resort for a while, but times were tough as the country was at war. They divided up the thousand-plus acres and sold off the parcels until eventually the remaining property was acquired by Judge C.W. Campbell, who demolished the resort buildings about 1927. Most of the ownership details in this book are placed in tables to spare the reader excessive detail while establishing a well-documented record (see Chapters 1-3, 5, and 7-9)

Most of the buildings familiar from pictures of Red Sulphur were built quite early. The iconic pavilion that contained the spring was erected in 1830 by James Harvey and this contained the spring. Burke however, built the long hotel buildings soon after, called cottage rows, which resemble modern motels. Fortunately, he included in his books detailed descriptions, including dimensions, of each structure; and these may be compared with a painting done in 1836 by George Esten Cooke.

The mission of Red Sulphur was primarily as a health resort, rather than a vacation resort as were many of the Virginia springs. William Burke in fact visited the resort as a patient prior to buying it. The claim was that the Red Sulphur waters were an effective treatment for "consumption," later called tuberculosis. This claim dominated the advertising, which became awkward when the nature of the tubercle bacillus was discovered by Robert Koch in 1882, revealing the very contagious nature of the disease was revealed. Fortunately, vintage advertisements for Red Sulphur Springs are easy to locate and reproduce using Newspapers.com (see Bibliography, Part Two) and a number have been selected as illustrations in this book.

The most useful source materials on Red Sulphur Springs available today are the few hotel ledgers that have survived, as these give the day-to-day arrival of guests for various years. Some of these are preserved in the Monroe County Historical Society Museum. The earliest of these, 1827-29 is new to the collection, recently donated by Jim Costa. This earliest ledger predates the Wm. Burke building spree, when just a few log houses existed, and gives insight into the operation at this early stage. Later ledgers are used to compare the clientele before and after the Civil War when the resort was in full swing. The 1890-02 ledger is the letter file of the manager, that is, copies of letters sent to prospective visitors, for food items, or letters hiring employees; and these give insight into the daily running of the resort. The guests came from a wide geographic range, from Boston and New York on the northeast, and New Orleans and Memphis on the southwest.

Chapter Four of this book is devoted to tracing the routes travelers took and the mode of transport that was used as technology evolved in the mid-nineteenth century. Private carriages or simply horses were all that was available in earliest times. Then stagecoach networks were established, followed by steamboats, canal boats, and finally railroads. Four to five miles per hour would have been the average travel speed in early times and even when railroads came in, horses were used initially for power.

External influences on the economy will also be analyzed. For instance, successive cholera epidemics in the lowland south induced plantation owners to escape with their families to the resorts in the hills, having a positive effect on the local economy. For example, hotel buildings would be constructed to accommodate the overflow. By comparison, financial panics also came in cycles, but this would have had the opposite effect; the clientele would decline markedly, leaving the resort owners with lowered revenues. Still another important influence on the economy was the Civil War during which the resorts were briefly turned into hospitals and campgrounds for the war-weary soldiers (see Chapter Six).

Finally in Chapter Ten some attention will be given to the composition of Red Sulphur Springs water in the context of neighboring springs and the geological history that is behind this unique phenomenon.

The border county region of Virginia and West Virginia, the Valley & Ridge Province of the Appalachian Mountains, was deformed and uplifted during the collision of southern and northern continents about 260 million years ago. Plate Tectonic studies tell us that during this long interval, this portion of the North American plate was transported from tropical environments to the temperate zone and brought with it the evidence, mainly hot climate evaporitic deposits that would eventually provide the springs with their minerals. This tectonic zone is now being reactivated and uplifted, due possibly to the beginning phases of the reclosure of the Atlantic Ocean. It is the revival of the mountainous terrain that provides the topography for artesian flow and generation of the springs. Prior to modern medicine, these springs were relied on to cure or at best relieve the symptoms of a great variety of diseases.

Table 0.1 Principal Information Sources on Red Sulphur Springs with Annotations

Original Writings

Henry Huntt, 1839, *A Visit to the Red Sulphur Springs.* Huntt's pamphlet features sections on travel routes and his experiences with early visitors and their cures.

William Burke, 1846, *The Mineral Springs of the Virginias*, also, 1860, *Red Sulphur Springs.* Burke built Red Sulphur into a group of hotel buildings capable of holding 350 visitors and wrote about the experience in detail and with many quotable passages as will be seen.

Newspapers.com. This website allows articles from the 1800's on to be found and printed, and these contain ads for the springs, stagecoach & train schedules, letters to the editors, etc.

Modern Materials

John W. Dumont, 1987, *Red Sulphur Springs Background Report.* This 46-page typescript paved the way for an archaeological study (see O'Malley below) and is the most complete account available.

Oren F. Morton, 1916, *A History of Monroe County.* This standard has just 2 pages on Red Sulphur but information on individuals associated with the Springs is found throughout.

Charles Motley, 1973, *Gleanings of Monroe County.* This useful reference has one detailed and very useful chapter on Red Sulphur Springs.

Nancy O'Malley, 1988, *Taking the Waters; Archaeological Investigations.* This report reviews and interprets the Native American artifacts discovered in the area.

Unpublished Ledgers (Monroe County Historical Society Collections)

John Hinton, Manager, 1827-1829. This Day Book has key information on some of the visitors when Red Sulphur consisted of just log structures, but it does not give their home states.

Red Sulphur Registers, 1834-6 and 1867-74. This collection is drawn from loose pages that have survived and they do give the home states of visiting parties.

Dunlap & Co. Store, 1849-51. This store was located adjacent to the Resort and served local farming families as well as visitors to the resort.

Dr. J.K.P. Gleeson Letter file, 1890-1892. This is a bound letter-file of the resort manager. It reveals the traveling plans of many visitors as well as interesting food items that were ordered for the table and diverse carriage types that were available to the guests for local drives in the country.

Monroe County Courthouse Records

Deeds, Trust-Deeds, and Wills are well indexed, representing the last 220 years and are critical to reconstructing the ownership history of the Red Sulphur Springs resort.

A complete list of resources is provided in the Bibliography.

Chapter 1

Nicholas Harvey and The Early Days of the Springs, 1795-1826

"Among the numerous advantages bestowed on Virginia by a bountiful Providence, there are perhaps none more important than the salubrity of climate and rich profusion of mineral waters of its transmontane territory. The happy combinations of these blessings, added to its central position, will not only make Western Virginia the great Mecca of invalid pilgrims, but its pellucid fountains, its beautiful villas, its secluded glens and majestic mountains, and the rich drapery of its noble forests, will ever attract to it the admirers of Nature's own workmanship." (Wm. Burke, 1846, *The Mineral Springs of Western Virginia*, p.12)

Discovery, 1795

Nicholas Harvey initially owned over 500 acres in the fertile Rich Creek Valley when he stumbled across Fitz Creek, a tributary of the adjacent Indian Creek drainage system about 1795. He must have given up farming at this point because Fitz Run Valley is just 150 feet wide and its floodplain is shouldered by 300-foot walls—too narrow for full sunlight, let alone crops. Yet he bought up five tracts around here in seven years, including the Red Sulphur Springs tract (Table 1.1). The Fitz Run valley is over an hour's horseback ride from his place on Rich Creek, so from age forty on he shifted his life's work to developing a resort here. His two teenage sons, James and John, must have helped; and eventually James inherited the property, as will be seen in Chapter Two.

Dr. William Burke also had a productive turn at running The Red, and he wrote down a lot of the earlier history in a most entertaining fashion, so we turn to him at various points in this narrative for his insights. In fact, in 1828 Burke visited the place as an invalid, when it was still in the log cabin stage. He found, "...a gloomy gorge skirted by dense forests and torn by contending torrents. A few comfortless cabins studded the little glen. No light was to be seen, for those cabins had no windows. A solitary light gleamed under the rude shelter that covered the Springs. All around seemed desolate and cheerless. Nor did the morn bring on its wings a brighter prospect: it only served to make darkness visible. The sun shone brilliantly, but it shone not upon the inhabitants of that valley. When it nearly reached the meridian, then only did it vouchsafe its

Table 1.1 Events in the Life of Nicholas Harvey, 1755-1826

1755. Born of John & Margaret Harvey, Orange Co., Northern Virginia (Clark, 1981, p.57).

1776? Served in the American Revolution (Clark, 1999).

1784. Moved with wife Sarah Ann and family to Greenbrier Co. (now Monroe County) (Shuck, 1988, p.145).

1785. Harvey had 100 acres surveyed on Rich Creek (Monroe Co. Survey Book 3, p.166).

1787. Was appointed an Overseer of Roads (Shuck, 1988, p.173) and served as an Ensign in the Militia under Capt. Hugh Caperton (Morton, 1916, p.267).

1792. Bought 400 acres on Rich Creek from Thomas and Ann Edgar for 5 shillings (Greenbrier Co. Deed Book 1, p.274) and had it surveyed in 1797 when it proved to hold 433 acres (Monroe Co. Survey Book 3, p.96).

1795. Had property surveyed on Fitz Run, Red Sulphur area (Monroe Co. Survey Bk. 3, p. 85) and by 1800 obtained a deed on 140 acres for this property (Monroe Co. Deed Bk. A, p.98). This area was an hour's horseback ride from his property on Rich Creek.

1797. Harvey had 152 acres surveyed on Indian Creek, near the mouth of Fitz Run and later identified as the Red Sulphur Springs Tract (Monroe Co. Deed Bk. 3, p.95; Clark, 1999).

1798. Surveyed 39 acres on Indian Creek adjoining his earlier land (Monroe Co. Survey Bk. 3, p.108).

1800. Bought 100 acres on Dogwood Flat, adjacent to the Red Sulphur Springs tract, from Thomas & Jenny Kirkpatrick (Monroe Co. Deed Bk. A, p.181).

1801. Harvey bought 554 acres on Indian Creek from Hugh and Rhoda Caperton for 10 pounds and recorded a deed (Deed Bk. A. p.188). This was later surveyed in 1804 and found to have 490 acres (Monroe County Survey Bk. 1, P.169). The total acreage acquired in the Red Sulphur Springs—Fitz Run—Indian Creek contiguous area encompassed 985 acres at this time.

1802. Dr. John Cabell of Lynchburg VA was the first person on record to visit the Spring for disease of the throat (Huntt, 1839, p.21, quoting James Harvey).

1821. Early record of case of "pulmonary consumption" (tuberculosis) treated at the Spring (Huntt, 1839, p.29).

1826. Nicholas died and was buried in the Harvey Cemetery at his homeplace on Pleasant Hill Farm (Shumate et al., 1990, p.200) across Indian Creek from the Red Sulphur Springs resort.

rays, and before the afternoon meal was ended, it again disappeared behind the Western forests" (Burke, 1846, pp.321-2).

The real discovery of Red Sulphur was most likely by Native Americans who roamed these hills over thousands of years, including along the Indian Creek Trail which that passed within a half mile of the Springs (Ziegler, 2019, p.116). This trail was part of a system that crossed the Appalachian Mountains and connected the Ohio and Shenandoah River Valleys. An archaeological search in the Fitz Creek Valley with shovel probes was not fruitful, but the adjacent Indian Creek area has yielded a "fairly dense lithic and ceramic scatter" dating from the Late Archaic Period (O'Malley, 1988, p.48). A more recent study upstream near Greenville at the Cook's Fort site yielded artifacts dating back to the Early Archaic Period, 6,900 B.C. (McBride & McBride, 2021, p.118). So Native Americans were using the trail at this early period. However, the main Red Sulphur Spring has a strong sulphureous odor which must have discouraged usage. Also, unlike most, this spring was apparently not a 'buffalo or deer lick' that is, it did not develop a saline deposit which would have encouraged game as well as early hunters of this ready source of meat (Ziegler, ibid., p.5-6).

Red Sulphur and The Neighboring Mineral Springs

The resort springs commonly mentioned with Red Sulphur in this part of the border-counties of the Virginias are listed in Table 1.2 together with dates and general comparisons. The West Virginia ones are located on Figure 1.1 The springs share a common geological environment, being within an ancient mountain range that is in the process of being actively uplifted and consequently down-cut or incised by river and stream erosion, and being in a zone of above-average precipitation. The scientific background for this, together with the evidence, is provided in Chapter Ten, along with the chemical variation in the springs and their relation to the geological formations. In the nineteenth and late eighteenth centuries the chemical composition of the spring water was touted to be crucial in curing a myriad of afflictions; in fact, published guides to the springs were dominated by testimonies of patients purported to be cured of various diseases. There can be no doubt that the cool mountain air, the relaxed atmosphere, and the diverse visitors had a salutary effect, but modern medicine has moved in a totally different direction, and the reader is herein spared all but a few short expositions of the nineteenth-century savants!

The eight resorts listed in Table 1.2 straddle the two Virginias. The ones closest to the stateline are within the zone of rock-deformation; that is, they are faulted and steeply folded with individual strata dipping vertically or even overturned. This is the result of the convergence and collision of the North American paleocontinent with Gondwanaland which terminated about 260 million years ago. The resorts of Red Sulphur, Salt Sulphur, and Blue Sulphur lie to the west of the deformed belt and contain the top of a relatively flat-lying sediment stack that is several miles thick; these deposits are referred to by geologists as platform-deposits and geomorphologically speaking, form the Allegheny Plateau region of much of West Virginia and other states along this zone. Both fold-belt and the immediate foreland, which contains the mineral springs, are involved in the fore mentioned presently active uplift zone. The area of faulting is important to note because here there are readymade channels to conduct rainwater to considerable depths and return with warm to hot waters due to the earth's heat flow. The idea here is that the natural thermal expansion would drive the water back to the surface.

The adventurous souls who developed these resorts, and the year about which this occurred, are also listed in Table 1.2. The Hot Springs and Warm Springs of Virginia were developed first simply because this area was settled first. In fact, as early as 1750 Dr. Thomas Walker, in his exploration of areas to the west,

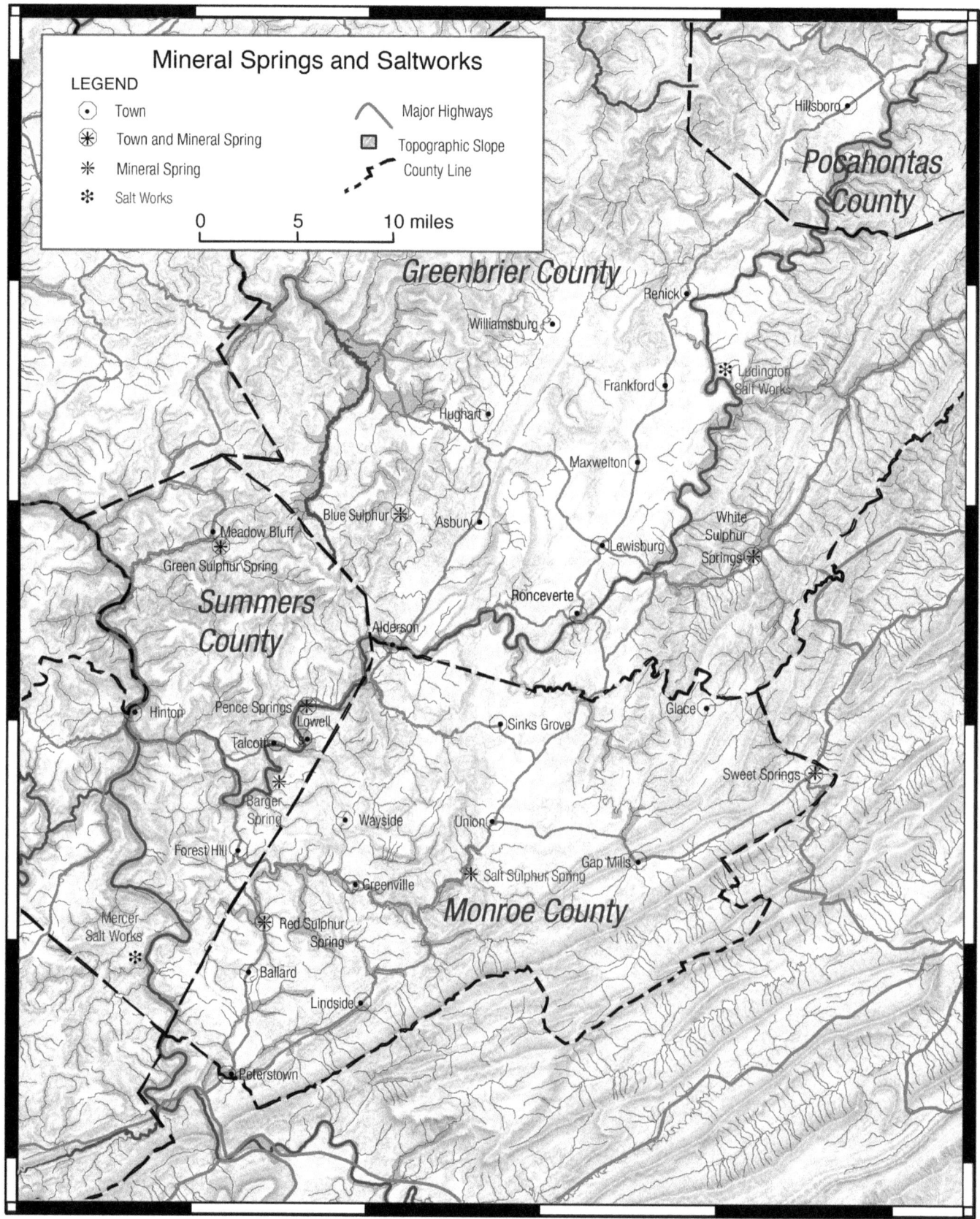

Figure 1.1 - Map of Monroe and Greenbrier Counties Showing Local Mineral Springs

returned east and wrote on July 9, "We went to the Hot Springs and found six invalids there. The spring water is very clear and warmer than new milk, and there is a spring of cold water within 20 feet of the warm one." So these springs were being used before the surrounding resorts were built. Also, in the category of warmer than average would be White Sulphur Springs and Sweet Springs. These are all in the deformed belt, suggesting that the water has the chance to circulate deeper where the fault zones are prevalent. Two of the springs, Grey and Blue Sulphur were developed late, and these did not survive the Civil War, so they were in business during the heyday of the springs but had a curtailed history. The various springs were important for each other because many of the visitors would patronize several during one trip, spending a week or so at each. People looking for a cure made the trip as well as people escaping the heat and low-land diseases, like cholera, in the South.

Table 1.2 - Local Resort Comparison (RSS Local Resort Comparison)

Name of Resort	Developer and Year	Location in County	Geology and Terrain	Reference, Date/Page
Grey Sulphur Springs	John D. Legare, 1834	North Giles, VA	Deformed Mountainous	L. Martindale, 2017, p. 77
Red Sulphur Springs	Nicholas Harvey, 1795	West Monroe, WV	Unfolded Hills	F. Ziegler, This Work
Salt Sulphur Springs	Ervan Benson, 1816	Central Monroe, WV	Unfolded Hills	J.R. Kidd, 1954, p. 187
Sweet Springs	William Lewis, 1785	East Monroe, WV	Deformed Mountains	A.E. Gish, 2009, p. 11
White Sulphur Springs	Michael Bowyer, 1784	Southeast Greenbrier, WV	Deformed Mountains	R.S. Conte, 1998, p. 4
Blue Sulphur Springs	George H. Buster, 1834	Southwest Greenbrier, WV	Unfolded Hills	I.S. Cadle, 2019, p. 4
Hot Springs	Thomas Bullitt, 1766	Central Bath, WV	Deformed Mountains	S. Cohen, 1984, p. 9
Warm Springs	John Lewis, 1761	Central Bath, WV	Deformed Mountains	S. Cohen, 1984, p. 19

Records of Early Usage of the Red Sulphur Springs

James Harvey was interviewed by Dr. Henry Huntt for his pamphlet, *A Visit to the Red Sulphur Spring of Virginia During the Summer of 1837*. This interview covers the visitors in the earliest years and in it he continued, "...that he had lived at and about the place for upwards of forty-three years (since 1794-5). The Spring was first visited by the neighbors for itch, sore legs, and other inveterate diseases of the skin, which were always cured by drinking the water and rubbing the parts affected with the muddy deposits. About thirty-six years ago (1802), Dr. John Cabell, of Lynchburg, Va., was the first person who visited the Spring for a cough, and disease of the throat, attended with chills and fevers. He remained here several weeks and returned home much better."

"The next season (continued Harvey), several other persons came, with cough and every appearance of consumption (tuberculosis). Afterwards, the number of visitors afflicted with this disease increased every year. There are many persons now living, within my knowledge, and enjoying excellent health, who visited this Spring many years ago, to all appearances in the last stage of consumption. The visitors who were

Table 1.3 Resort Furniture, Dishes, and Bedroom Equipment, 1826

Nicholas Harvey Estate Appraisement, (Monroe Co. Will Bk. 2, pp.349-352)
Shortened from 4-page original (T.N. Clark, 1999)

Bedroom Supplies
28 Bedsteads with 'chords'
   (ropes supporting the mattresses)
8 Bedsteads & Furniture
24 Cot Frames
30 Chamber Pots, 25 Pitchers, & 42 Bowls
58 Counterpins (bedspreads)
77 Sheets (10 linen)
68 Bed Ticks (Mattresses)
56 Pillows (23 goose & 11 hen feathers)
18 Bolsters (10 feather & 8 straw)
26 Pillowcases
42 Indian Blankets
29 Candle Sticks & 21 Candle Snuffers
14 Looking Glasses

Dining Room Equipment
70 Knives, Forks, & Spoons
   (12 with ivory handles)
5 Walnut Dining Room Tables
1 Walnut "Fall Leaf" Table
23 Small Tables
84 Chairs
Teacups & Saucers
Glass Tumblers & Stemware
China Plates & Earthen Plates
Waiters & Castor Stands
   (tabletop serving devices?)
Salt Cellars & Mustard Pots

most benefited by the water, remained here five or six weeks; confined themselves to a diet of rye mush and milk; and were industrious in rising early, drinking the water and taking exercise. Others who indulged themselves in eating, sleeping late in the morning, and lounging about during the day, derived but little advantage from the use of the water, and generally returned home dissatisfied. The cold plunging, or shock bath, was used in those days with decided advantage. I never knew a case injured by the use of the cold bath."

"Many cases of dropsy (edema) visited the spring, and I never knew of an instance where they were not relieved by the use of the water. One of my neighbors was cured many years ago by the use of this water, and now enjoys excellent health. I have known many persons affected with complaints of the liver and bowels completely relieved by the Red Sulphur Water. From the first of May to the middle of November is the proper time for using the water to advantage, but I think it strongest in its various virtues during the months of September to October." Thus ended the interview with James Harvey. It shows well the development of the idea that the Red Sulphur water was an effective treatment for consumption, or at least for relieving its symptoms.

The Will of Nicholas Harvey, 1826

Nicholas owned Red Sulphur for about thirty years and his will and appraisal of his belongings have been summarized by his descendant, Thomas N. Clark (1981, 1999). It seems that both Nicholas and son James lived at Pleasant Hill Farm on Indian Creek, across from Red Sulphur Springs, evidently their abode for all thirty years because this is where both generations are buried. Although ownership of the Springs was divided between James and his brother John, James was to have the renting and selling of the springs at his disposal. Clark felt that John was regarded as somewhat of a spendthrift by the father and, in any case, John seems to have moved away to Kanawha County at an early stage.

The Estate Appraisement of Nicholas was reworked by Clark (Table 1.3) and he interpreted this data to indicate that the resort could accommodate as many as fifty visitors by the time of Nicholas' death. We assume that the number fifty included the visitor's slaves and that they were assigned the cots while their owners slept on the bedsteads and mattresses. Also, it must be remembered that it was customary at the time in hotels for several people, including strangers, to sleep together in one bed. So the number fifty may be an overestimate as ledger data that survives from the years that James owned the hotel will show in the following chapter. Nicholas' will states that he passed on to son John one negro boy named John, and to James one negro girl named Nancy, so the number of slaves used to run the resort may have been small.

Red Sulphur Springs, West Virginia

Chapter 2

James Harvey, the Pavilion, and Some Early Visitor Records 1826-1832

We have seen that the father, Nicholas, devoted the last thirty years of his life to Red Sulphur Springs, and the son James was there for at least the first thirty of his mature years. However, James' heart may not have been in this business as he sold the resort just seven years after inheriting it; and he deferred the running of the business to a local gentleman, John Hinton, who rented the establishment for the years, 1827-29. James had the good taste to build the iconic classical-style pavilion over the spring in 1830 before selling the resort in 1832. The Hinton years survive in the form of a detailed ledger, and the pavilion survives in numerous photos taken over a hundred-year period.

The Iconic Pavilion

William Burke, subsequent owner, wrote the following, "...the structure most deserving of notice is the Pavilion over the Springs (Figure 2.1). This beautiful edifice was erected in 1830 after a design of Mr. Strickland of Philadelphia. It is a dome 42 feet in diameter, supported by 12 ionic columns. The height from the base to the top of the entablature is about 30 feet. The Springs rise 10 feet beneath the natural level of the valley, and their depth being over 4 feet, you descend 5½ feet by circular steps. The whole height from the level of the water to the top of the dome is about 50 feet. The Springs rise horizontally in two marble reservoirs. They derive their name from a rich lake-colour deposit which is sometimes seen in large quantities on the sides of the fountains. Their waters are conducted into a wooden reservoir in the center, and thence by pipes to the bathing-house" (1846, p.185).

Architect William Strickland (1788-1854) helped establish the Greek Revival Movement in the United States, and some of his most famous works are in Philadelphia and in Nashville, Tennessee, where he later lived. The nature of the red color of the spring water is the subject of eight pages of text (Burke, 1846, p.187-196) but has apparently never been adequately determined. Normally, the red color in water would be assumed to be due to the presence of iron and the word "chalybeate" applied, but although some

Table 2.1 Events in the Life of James Harvey, 1782-1866

1794. Moved to Red Sulphur Springs with parents Nicholas and Sarah Ann Harvey (Huntt, 1839, p.21).

1799. Served in the Monroe County Militia (Clark, 1981, p. 60).

1813. Married Nancy Snidow in adjacent Giles County, VA in 1813 (Clark, 1981, p.60).

1822. Acquired 140 acres on Indian Creek from his parents Nicholas and Sarah for $400 (Monroe County Deed Book G., p.547).

1826. With his brother John inherited Red Sulphur Springs on the death of their father, Nicholas. The will indicates that James was to manage the hotel business, and that there were sufficient beds and dishes at this time for 50 people (Clark, 1999).

1827. Rented out the hotel, which consisted of several log houses, to John Hinton who then managed the business for three years (Original Day Book; Jim Costa).

1828. James D. Legare, future owner of the Grey Sulphur Springs resort, visited Red Sulphur during the summer (Day Book; Costa).

1829. William Burke, future owner attended Red Sulphur as a patient and at this time must have met John D. Legare, also visiting this year (Day Book; Costa).

1830. James Harvey had the signature pavilion erected over the Spring (Burke, 1846, p.16).

1832. James and John sold the Red Sulphur Springs resort to William Burke. (Burke, 1846, p.186) The deal was supported by a Trust Deed held by trustees Andrew Beirne and Conway Robinson (Motley, 1973, p.127).

1866. Died and was buried at the family home, Pleasant Hill Farm, just across Indian Creek from Red Sulphur Springs (Clark, 1981, p.61; Shumate, 1990, p.200).

iron is present, the red color seems to be due to a peculiar red organic substance instead (Ziegler, 2014, 8; McColloch, 1986, p.262).

Wm. Burke provides a general description of the spring water follows; "This water is perfectly colorless and transparent; when agitated it has an agreeable sparkling appearance. Its odor is that of hydro-sulphuric acid, mixed with that from earth or clay; the latter being retained, after the hydro-sulphuric acid is dissipated, or destroyed. Its taste is hepatic (liver-like) and slightly bitter. By ebullition (bubbling), it does not immediately become turbid, gases escape, and when reduced in volume by evaporation deposition takes place." (Burke, 1846, p.17) The guests were urged to drink this water and to bathe in it, but it certainly does not sound very appetizing or pleasant to smell. This may explain why Native Americans seem to have avoided the spring, as mentioned earlier. For a general description of the various spring-water types, see Appendix Four.

Figure 2.1 - Spring House Built in 1830.

The John Hinton Ledger

John Hinton (1788-1858) is best known as one of the founders of Hinton, county seat of neighboring Summers County; however, he grew up near Greenville in Monroe County and was hired as a young man by James Harvey to manage the resort from 1827-29. It seems that he later moved to a site on the Greenbrier River, set up a ferry business and probably an adjacent store by the river, and was there when the new county of Summers was founded in the 1870's. We learn these details from a day book kept by Hinton and preserved by Jim Costa, local collector and history buff, as well as from Miller's *History of Summers County* (1908, p.533).

Hinton's ledger is unusually detailed except it does not include the region from which the guests came, so we must wait until later chapters to be impressed by the extent of travel of many of the visitors. But, here are some of the economic details of running a country resort nearly two hundred years ago:

Yearly Rent	Season Length	Days Open
1827, $300.00	12 Jul—19 Sep	70 days
1828, $450.00	24 May—28 Sep	128 days
1829, $477.00	17 Jun—13 Oct	126 days

Daily charges were: $1.00/day/guest, $0.50/day/servant, $0.50/day/horse, and $0.06 ¼ to wash one piece of clothing.

The following statistics are based on the 1827 season although we note that it was quite a bit shorter than the subsequent two. The summary data set is presented in Table 2.2 and is organized by date of arrival. Note that asterisks are used to indicate guests who returned for a visit later in the season. The total amount paid includes laundry in addition to the fees for the guests, servants and horses; and the grand total taken in was $1,352.58. A significant fact is that each of the parties arrived with horses, whether it be one, two or three. Single travelers would have come on horseback, while larger parties would have brought carriages. There was no public transportation in the form of stagecoaches hinted at and no trains in this early dataset. All of this would change in the following decades, as will be seen.

Figure 2.2 provides the number of parties as well as the number of people through the season using a weekly frequency. The maximum number of people was 33 and occurred on August 1. These numbers pale by comparison with the 1830's when the Burke building boom occurred. Figure 2.3 shows the length of stay according to the number of parties and we see the largest numbers staying just a week or two - these were the guests "doing the spring circuit" - while the longest stays of three to four weeks must have been by the seriously ill patients. There were a number of visits of one or two days by one person, and these were probably the "gay young blades" out for a party.

An interesting sidelight in Hinton's ledger is that two future resort developers visited Red Sulphur, presumably during the time that they formed the idea to go into the business and indeed made local arrangements to do so. The first was in 1828, when John D. Legare of Charleston, South Carolina, visited on five separate occasions for a total of 56 days. He came back in 1829 for another five visits and this time spent a total of 66 days. He would go on to develop the Grey Sulphur Springs, eight miles south of Red Sulphur, in adjacent Giles County but very close to Peterstown in Monroe County. During his 1929 visits he would have met William Burke of Richmond, Virginia who spent 18 days at The Red as an invalid. Burke would go on to buy The Red and spend $100,000.00 in developing it, His ownership was by far the most significant period in its long history.

Table 2.2 - Data from the Hinton Ledger for 1827 - part 1
(some names appear twice because they made two visits)

Name	Arrive	Leave	Days	Men	Wom.	Child.	Serv.	Horse	Paid	Pg.
Alfred Lewis	12-Jul	24-Jul	13	1	1		2	2	$59.50	1
Rob. Hampton	14-Jul	18-Jul	5	1				1	$6.00	2
Carlina Nicholson	14-Jul	18-Jul	5		1			1	$6.50	3
Martin Slaughter	15-Jul	14-Aug	31	1				1	$43.80	4
Paul J. Tardy	15-Jul	11-Aug	28	1				1	$41.50	5
Thos. Walker	15-Jul	12-Aug	29	1				1	$47.50	6
H. Tines	18-Jul	8-Aug	22	1			1	2	$54.50	7
L. Mitchell	18-Jul	19-Jul	2	1				1	$2.54	8
George Burrill	18-Jul	19-Jul	2	1				1	$3.34	9
Thos. Hooper	20-Jul	28-Jul	9	1			1	2	$21.17	10
Phillip Payne	22-Jul	15-Aug	25	1	1		2	3	$90.00	11
Wm. W. Austin	22-Jul	14-Aug	24	1	1		1	2	$84.87	12
Joseph Wilson	22-Jul	24-Jul	3	1				1	$4.50	13
John McCormick	23-Jul	24-Jul	2	1				1	$1.75	15
John Rose	25-Jul	26-Jul	2	1				1	$3.49	16
Rich P. Watson	27-Jul	10-Aug	15	1	1		1	1	$42.19	17
John Gist	29-Jul	23-Aug	26	1				1	$39.68	18
Freeman Walker	29-Jul	22-Aug	25	1	1		1	2	$93.75	19
Henry Malone	29-Jul	22-Aug	25	1	1		1	1	$85.00	20
J.B. Herbert	29-Jul	4-Aug	7	1			1	1	$13.40	21
John McKim	30-Jul	3-Aug	5	1	1	2	3	3	$28.00	22
Ben B. Watson	30-Jul	9-Aug	11	1				1	$16.00	23
H.T. Harrison	1-Aug	4-Aug	4	1				1	$4.50	2
Robert Young	2-Aug	21-Aug	20	1				1	$23.25	2

Table 2.2 - Data from the Hinton Ledger for 1827 - part 2

Name	Arrive	Leave	Days	Men	Wom.	Child.	Serv.	Horse	Paid	Pg.
Fred Montgomery	5-Aug	21-Aug	16	1	2		1	3	$70.68	1
Hugh R. Morris	10-Aug	24-Aug	15	1				1	$21.68	3
John W. Carvile	10-Aug	25-Aug	16	1			1	2	$16.37	4
Newton Marke	17-Aug	21-Aug	5	1			1	1	$12.18	17
Alex Winstead	20-Aug	26-Aug	7	1	1		1	2	$28.27	12
John Madison	22-Aug	24-Aug	3	1				1	$3.50	11
David Wilson	23-Aug	1-Sep	10	1				1	$13.50	3
G. Cooper	23-Aug	1-Sep	10	1	1		2	3	$40.50	5
Jone Royall	23-Aug	9-Sep	18		1	2	2	2	$68.00	9
Abram Sydnor	27-Aug	19-Sep	24	1				1	$35.49	8
H. Tines	27-Aug	13-Sep	18	1			1	3	$48.14	7
T. Fantain	28-Aug	3-Sep	7	1				1	$9.37	11
J.P. Scrugs	30-Aug	3-Sep	5	2				1	$11.50	15
Allen Wilson	31-Aug	2-Sep	3	1		1		1	$5.00	16
Newton Marke	31-Aug	8-Sep	9	1				1	$12.00	17
Gestaves Deep	31-Aug	2-Sep	3	1				1	$3.00	20
Alex Winstead	1-Sep	13-Sep	12	1				1	$18.00	12
H.C. Belcher	4-Sep	14-Sep	11	1			1	2	$33.30	10
Thos. B. Coleman	5-Sep	9-Sep	5	1	1		1	2	$11.50	13
W.J. Myddleton	9-Sep	14-Sep	6	1			1	3	$21.00	9
Mrs. Havesham	9-Sep	14-Sep	6		2		1	2	$19.50	10
R.D. Palmer	9-Sep	16-Sep	8	1	1			1	$18.00	15
H. Graham	11-Sep	14-Sep	4	2				2	$9.12	11
W.B. Ceebrook	12-Sep	16-Sep	5	1				a	$6.25	19

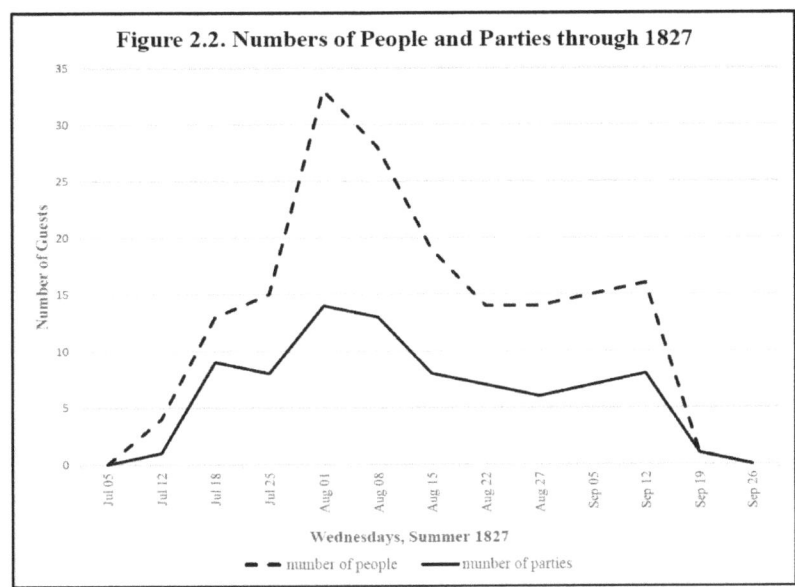

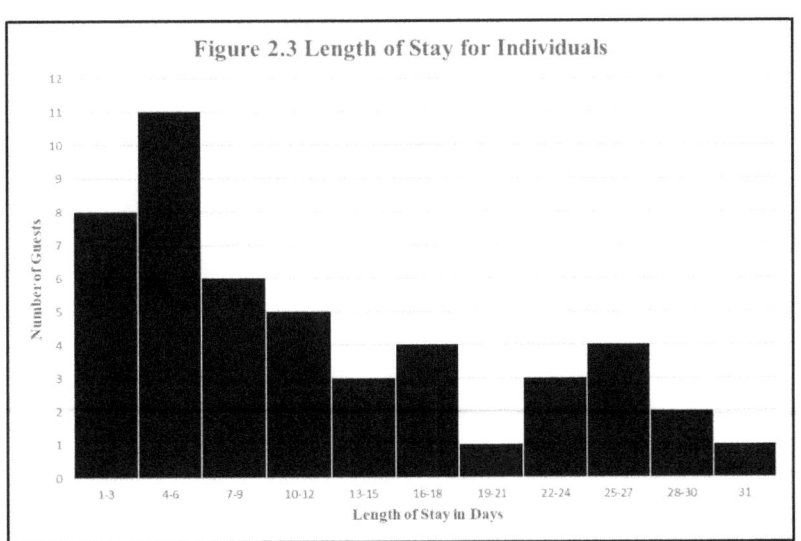

Travel and Communications within the Virginia Springs

In writing this book, great use was be made of the new computer webb site "Newspapers.com" (see Bibliography, Part 2) and an early example from this source is an April, 1825 article from the Charleston Courier of South Carolina. It is from an advertisement for Botetourt Springs, which was just north of the later town of Roanoke, Virginia, and gives insight into travel at this early date. In fact, a careful search shows it to be the very first mention of Red Sulphur Springs on this webb site. The first paragraph talks about travel and the second about receiving mail on a trip around the Virginia Springs.

"Gentlemen from the South wishing to dispense with the use of Carriages and Horses, can come directly to the spot without incurring the expense of either—they will proceed by water from Charleston or any other southern port to Norfolk, thence in the Steam-boat to Richmond, from whence there is twice a week a Mail Stage that now passes within two miles of this place, and after the 15th June will come directly to the spot, passing through the flourishing town of Lynchburg. After arriving here and remaining as long as agreeable, they can then proceed to any other of the adjacent Springs they may choose, in a hack kept by the Subscriber for that purpose. The distance to the Sweet Springs is thirty-seven miles—to the White Sulphur 55—to the Sweet and Salt Sulphur 60—to the Red Sulphur 72—and to the Hot and Warm Springs, between 60 and 70 miles."

"It is recommended to gentlemen intending to visit any of the Virginia Watering Places to have their letters addressed to the Botetourt Springs, it being the first watering place they will touch at in going, and the last in returning. They will experience great convenience in following those directions; because, on their arrival they may find letters from home, and during their stay, will have an opportunity of hearing from their friends every other day, as the Mail from the South arrives three times a week, whereas at all other Springs it is believed to arrive only once a week. If, after remaining with the Subscriber as long as agreeable, they should choose to proceed to any of the neighboring Springs, he promises that their letters shall be carefully forwarded whithersoever they may direct."

It is clear from this article that the people going to the Springs would travel from as far away as Charleston, South Carolina, then some 450 miles by sea, 100 miles by steamboat on the lower James River, another 150 miles by stage to Botetourt, and finally 72 miles on to Red Sulphur in a hack (small carriage). So, the total mileage would have been 772 miles while the actual straight-line distance would have been about 340 miles. Direct stage service would have been possible, but the ocean and river boat route may have been as quick as travel would have been round-the-clock. Altogether, time consumed in travel one-way would have been a week at least as we shall see in subsequent chapters.

Chapter 3

William Burke, Builder and Promoter
1832-1842

"The Red Sulphur Springs came into my possession in the autumn of 1832 by purchase" (Burke, 1846, p.186). "It would be difficult to conceive a spot better calculated to discourage an attempt at improvement, and indeed many had declared it impracticable to any extent. Such, however, was not our opinion; we were aware that it was only necessary to follow, rather than to subdue nature, and that by doing so we might make something interesting out of this wild and unpromising gorge. It is not too much to say that the result has corresponded with our anticipations, and that whether as a whole or in detail, this little valley may compare favourably with any merely rural scene in America."

Burke's Background

Burke is traditionally thought of as a medical doctor, but prior to buying Red Sulphur he was Principal of the Richmond Seminary for 13 years (*Richmond Enquirer*, 1830); in 1830, Christianna, his wife organized a parallel institution, the Richmond Female Seminary that would receive "daily assistance from Mr. Burke." This institution would admit young ladies as boarders and scholars and "enable them to all the advantages in this State, and not inferior to those of any Northern Institution." The list of course offerings is impressive; *Orthography, Reading, Writing, English Grammar, Elocution, Belles Lettres, Epistalary Style, Ancient & Modern History, Geography, with the use of Globes and Maps, Astronomy, Natural History, Botany, Arithmetic, Bookkeeping, Algebra, Geometry, Natural Philosophy, Chemistry, The Greek, Latin, French, Italian and Spanish Languages, Vocal and Instrumental Music, Drawing and Painting and Dancing*. This list demonstrates that the Burkes went well beyond range of the word seminary. Additional teachers were brought in to handle the math and foreign language courses. Somehow, William also found time to publish an edition of *Adam's Latin Grammar* (*Richmond Enquirer*, 1833). So, the Burkes were heavily into education before acquiring Red Sulphur.

The Burkes had at least two children, but all we know about them is that there was a girl who played music and sang with her mother at Red Sulphur and a son, Dr. Thomas J. Burke, who had 18 years of professional

Table 3.1 Events in the Life of William Burke

1829. William Burke visited Red Sulphur Springs in August as an invalid (Burke, 1860, p.3; Logbook of John Hinton).

1830. Burke and wife, Christianna were running schools in Virginia, the Richmond Male Seminary and Female Seminary respectively (*Richmond Enquirer*, Aug 10, 1830).

1832. Burke bought Red Sulphur Springs on a Trust Deed held by Andrew Beirne and Conway Robinson (Deed Bk. K, p.299).

1832. The Cholera Epidemic hit the coastal South, stimulating plantation owners to escape to the mountain resorts for the summer (Pyle, 1969, p.63) and providing more business for the resort springs (Reniers, 1941, p.74).

1833. Burke demolished the original log houses and replaced them with elegant hotel structures, and he also cleared much of the forest (Burke, 1846, p.186-7). The hotel was completed for this season and accommodations increased to 150 persons (*National Gazette*, Philadelphia May 22, 1833).

1833. Burke published an edition of Adam's Latin Grammar, "with important additions from the best authorities" (*National Gazette*, Jul 30, 1833).

1834. Burke continued to add buildings to Red Sulphur, increasing the capacity to 250, and even established a school at Red Sulphur for the education of young gentlemen (*Charleston Mercury*, Jun 30, 1834).

1836. The famous picture of these developments was painted by George Cooke looking north from Mt. Ida (Burke, 1846, p.186).

1836. The Red and Blue Sulphur Springs Turnpike Company was chartered, adding to the springs turnpike circuit system and to the comfort and speed of travel between the various resorts (Martindale, 2017, p.48).

1838. President Van Buren visited the Springs, including Red Sulphur, in September (*Richmond Enquirer*, Sep 28, 1838).

1841. Wm. Burke and Christianna reopened the Richmond Seminary, the school for young men and ladies (*Richmond Enquirer*, Oct 15, 1841).

1841. Red Sulphur was opened by James Dunlap, working for Wm. Burke (*Richmond Enquirer*, Jul 8, 1842).

1842. The Financial Panic of 1837 severely affected patronage at all resort spas and Burke was eventually forced to surrender the property in 1842 (Burke 1842, p.169).

1842. Wm. Burke published one of the first comprehensive books on the Virginia Springs, copies of which have been reprinted in recent times (Burke, 2nd ed., 1846).

experience at Red Sulphur (Univ. of Virginia, 2021). William returned to teaching at the Richmond Seminary in 1841 when he gave up ownership of Red Sulphur. By 1846 he had published the second edition of his book, a 394-page tome on *The Mineral Springs of Western Virginia* originally published in 1842. He was still publishing in 1860, this time a more modest book devoted just to Red Sulphur and written from Glennville in Barbour County, Alabama; this may have been his ancestral home. He was not part of the Burke family of Burkes Garden, in Tazewell County, Virginia, as has been assumed by some.

As previously mentioned, William Burke first visited Red Sulphur as an invalid in 1829 and bought it in 1832. The nature of his infliction is not stated but a good guess is that it was consumption, that is, tuberculosis in modern terms because he stressed the benefits of the water in treating this disease. However, it would be cholera would propel the Red Sulphur and the other springs' visitor base for the next four years.

"The Year of The Cholera"

The first of three cholera epidemics to hit North America was in 1832. The bacterium *Vibrio cholerae* had been endemic to the Ganges River of northeastern India since antiquity, but due to the colonization of the British in the eighteenth century and increased contact in the nineteenth century, it was carried to Europe in 1817 and again in 1830. It finally made the jump across the Atlantic by 1832. From New York on June 26 it moved to Richmond by July 6, to Charleston by late October, and to New Orleans by November 18 (Pyle, 1969); and all these cities sent visitors to Red Sulphur. This event was called an "epidemic," apparently because of delays caused by the length of intracontinental travel time, but it did infect much of the civilized globe, so it was in retrospect properly a "pandemic."

"Cholera did for the Springs what prosperity was not ready to do—sent them on a flying start on the decade" (Reniers, 1941, Chapter 5). The Springs did not treat the disease but rather gave harbor to those who were trying to escape it. Forty people died per day in Richmond, three quarters were slaves; so the plantation owners formed the habit of escaping to the mountain resorts with their families for the summer, spending a week or two at each of the Springs in succession. Cholera succeeded smallpox as one of the most dreaded disease in the United States and the burden of the suffering fell on the poor due to bad sanitation (Snowden, 2019, Chapter 13). The cholera epidemic years in North America were 1832, 1849, and 1866 (see Appendix On and Two). Over this period, it was realized that control of the drinking water was crucial in combating cholera, so the severity of the disease was gradually brought under control and terminated on this continent later in the century.

The Building Boom

Burke initially embarked on an ambitious building spree and in 1833 advertised "A spacious Hotel, one hundred and twelve by forty-two feet has been erected, which with its extensive porches and balconies, will afford much comfort and accommodation." In fact, during this first year of ownership he had expanded the capacity of the resort from 30 to 150 persons. He also boasted at this time:

"Baths affording water of any temperature desired, will always be in readiness."

"The beds, matrasses, bedding, and table furniture, are all new and of the best quality."

"The most celebrated Cook in Virginia has been engaged—and indeed all the servants have been selected with great care."

"A select library of miscellaneous works, together with periodicals, newspapers, &c. will be furnished."

Red Sulphur Springs.

THE improvements making at these celebrated Springs are very extensive. They will accommodate next season, with comfort, about two hundred and fifty persons. The astonishing influence possessed by these waters, in the cure of pulmonary diseases, and in the reduction of arterial action, is well known; indeed, they seem to afford the only hope in arresting Consumption, Dyspepsia, Chronic, Diarrhœa and Dissentery, Liver Complaints, Gravel, Dropsy, Rheumatism, Gout, Diseases of the Uterus, Neuralgia, Tremor, Syphilis, general Nervous Debility, Worms, Cutaneous Eruptions. These and other diseases have been cured or alleviated by the use of these waters. The establishment will be under the management of Major Wm Vass, whose disposition to please is well known. He is furnished with plentiful supplies, and some of the best servants in the State.— There is a Store, with a large capital, on the premises. A Seminary has been established here for the education of young gentlemen. The number of pupils is limited to thirty. The Seminary has the undivided attention of the undersigned; and of Mr James Macully as Teacher of Mathematics.

May 30   f4   WM. BURKE.

The editors of the Richmond Whig, Nat. Intelligencer, N Y. Courier and Enquirer, Nat. Gazette, and Baltimore American, are requested to insert the above once a week for four weeks, send their papers from the 1st July until 1st October, and transmit their accounts.

Figure 3.1 This advertisement was published as Red Sulphur was going through a ten-fold expansion. It includes claims that 17 diseases could be cured or at least alleviated through use of these waters. The final paragraph was intended for newspaper editors only and tells that the ads were directed to places in Virginia, District of Columbia, New York, Pennsylvania, Maryland, and South Carolina, a wide range, but it does not include Gulf Coastal States as does later advertising (*The Charleston, SC Mercury*, Jun 20, 1834).

Figure 3.2 - Copy of Painting of Red Sulphur Springs by George Eston Cooke in 1836.

"Music will be engaged, and such other amusements provided as are calculated to promote rational enjoyment and recreation."

"The best liquors, wines, groceries, and supplies of all kinds, have been provided in abundance."

"The stables have been extended, and first-rate ostlers have been engaged."

"The roads will be good, and the eastern mail will arrive daily in four-horse coaches, by way of the other Springs.

"Stages arrive three times a week from Wythe court-house, which will enable travelers from the south and west to come in by a direct route."

In advertisements for 1834 Burke put the accommodation number at 250 and introduced a seminary for young gentlemen along the lines of his former school in Richmond (Figure 3.1). In 1836, he brought in itinerant artist George Esten Cooke to document the resort in his famous painting (Figure 3.2); he added additional buildings in 1837 to handle a total of 300 guests, according to the newspapers.

All of this was recognized by visitors and the following anonymous detailed description appeared in 1837 in the Southern Literary Messenger (O'Malley, 1988, p.49) "The road from the Salt to the Red is greatly improved by several changes of location; and was, indeed, during the last summer, one of the best, if not the very best, in the mountains. The traveler may now take a stage at the White Sulphur after breakfast, dine at the Salt, and reach the Red early in the afternoon. The approach by mountain road, which crosses Indian Creek for the last time near Neel's tavern (to go up Hans Creek), six and a half miles from the Red, we think the most interesting and better road. Arrived at the summit of the eastern mountain (Kibble Hill), you soon reach a point from which an almost bird's-eye view of the valley bursts on your sight."

"After travelling through a country which abounds in magnificent natural scenery, but with rare marks of cultivation and none whatever of taste, such a scene cannot fail to inspire agreeable sensations. The road is conducted, as to bring in view the whole establishment before you reach the hotel: you wind around a lovely hill (Mount Ida), having a terrace promenade, immediately over the road, several rustic seats on the slope; and on its summit a platform raised to the branches of a spreading oak, intersected by convenient and judiciously planned walks, and overshadowed by numerous majestic sugar maples; the rich green sward forming a lovely contrast with the snow-white buildings and enclosure. Alabama row on the left is the first range of which a front view is presented: it is about three hundred feet long, forming a handsome crescent, and fronted with a colonnade the whole of its length: which, in case of damp or sunshine, affords a delightful promenade for its occupants. You next pass the spring, covered by an octagon building and surmounted by a set of huge elk-horns. On either side of it are two small grassplots which present a peculiarly neat appearance. You now reach the hotel, a spacious structure of two stories, extending in a direction from north to south about one hundred and twenty feet; the model of this building is highly imposing and picturesque, commanding from its ample porches a full view of all the premises and the different roads leading to the establishment. Immediately opposite, and at the base of the eastern hill, is a neat one-storied range of one hundred feet long, called Bachelor's Row, having a handsome portico, and designed, as its name denotes, for the accommodation of single gentlemen. At its upper extremity and connected by an arched way, is the much-admired Philadelphia Row, two hundred feet in length, with a beautiful portico fronting double rooms, intended for families. At the lower end, and also connected by a portico, is a newly erected receiving room fitted up with books, games and musical instruments, more especially designed as a private sitting room for ladies. A continuation of the portico connects with Carolina House, an elegant and chaste two-storied building, one hundred and twenty feet long, with double porticos on front and rear."

"The whole of the ranges just mentioned present a colonnade of four hundred and eighty feet in length. On a terrace, excavated to a depth of sixty feet, through solid rock, and immediately above Bachelor's Row, towers the newly erected and majestic edifice appropriately termed Society Hall; it is three stories high and eighty feet long; its portico, extending to the roof, is eighty feet long, is supported by nine columns of most exact architectural proportions. Extending down the valley is a beautiful oval lawn, around which the road diverges, one to the gateway and store, the other to the offices and stables."

The Society Hall seems to have been special and it was reviewed about 1840 by "James Silk Buckingham, one of the incoming mob of British journalists, who happened along about the time the doctor had reared his most magnificent gallery, and Mr. Buckingham declared flatly that between this place and Saratoga, the pride of the North, there was just no choice. The Red Sulphur could give Saratoga its powerful medicated water and still win, hands down. At Saratoga there was, said Mr. Buckingham, a hot, sandy, dusty town, hardly higher than the heat-stricken cities around it; there were five or six hotels under different management, 'all crowded to excess,' and at all of them there was a mad and disorderly rush for seats in the dining room").

"Here at Dr. Burke's there was no hot, sandy town, indeed no town at all, but a cool green valley and one commodious establishment with room for everybody. In the dining room there were only two hundred people in a space designed for three hundred; you were blessed with attentive waiters, place cards and, wonderful to behold, a series of those broad Southern fly fans hanging from the ceiling over the long tables, all connected so that one servant at the ropes could swing the lot of them at once" (as quoted in Reniers, 1941, p.98). The comment about the empty seats in the dining room was ominous and would hint at the fact that Burke would eventually be forced to give up all of this magnificence.

Finally, here are some words about Red Sulphur and Mr. Burke during the tour of the United States President, Martin Van Buren (*Richmond Enquirer*, 1838). "On Sunday, the President attended Divine Worship in Union, at the church of the Rev. Mr. Preston, and on Monday, departed for the Red Sulphur Springs, an excellent and truly desirable watering place, and is deservedly the favorite resort of both the invalid and the robust. The sublimity of the scenery, neatness of the buildings and enclosure, the unequalled and most remarkable quality of the water, and the urbanity of the worthy proprietor, Mr. Burke, together with his fine table, place this interesting retreat, I might almost say *primus inter pares"* (first among equals).

Where They Came From

Some information may be gained from miscellaneous ledger pages preserved in the records of the Monroe County Historical Society (Table 3.2). These pages represent the years 1834 and 1836, as well as several pages dating from after the Civil War which are discussed in Chapter Seven. These data pages give only the number of parties as a function of the city and/or state of origin, and not the total number of people or the duration of the visit. In 1834, the total was 664 parties, and in 1836 it was 897. These numbers therefore predate the "Financial Panic of 1837" that resulted in a drop in patronage at the Springs lasting for several years. So, 1836 should be considered a high point for the William Burke era.

The airline distances quoted in Table 3.2 are given as ranges representing different cities in each state unless just one city is found' in which case that single distance is shown. The states are listed in rough order from northeast to southwest, and it will be seen that the airline distances traveled may be up to 600 and even 750 miles. This seems to be quite remarkable, considering a significant portion of the travel would have been by stagecoach.

An example of a trip is that of Peregrine Prolix who published a meticulous account of his 1834 trip from Philadelphia to Warm Springs trip, which is, at the northeast end of the Springs circuit (Table 3.3). The airline distance would be about 220 miles to Warm Springs and 300 to Red Sulphur. It took four days to get to Warm Springs on the inbound trip and five on the outbound, with average speeds of 5.8 m.p.h. and 5.5

m.p.h. respectively. So it would have taken another two days coming and going to include Red Sulphur in the trip.

Stagecoach links were included in each day of travel except one, and each night was spent in an inn. However, most days were quite long, beginning as early as 3 or 4 a.m. and ending as late as 9:30 but usually with a long midday stop to have the main "dinner" of the day. Also, the average speeds were fastest on the days which included travel by water, be it sea, river, or canal. Rail travel was limited at this early time to just one leg of the trip, and the train was drawn by horses part of the time. In conclusion, travel was obviously very time consuming, and an easy day trip today would have taken a week in the 1830s. Because of the revolution in transportation in the mid-nineteenth century, Chapter Four in this book will be devoted entirely to this subject.

Table 3.2 - Visitor Travel Data for 1836 and 1869

Airline Distance to Red Sulphur	1836 % Parties	State of Origin North to South	1869 % Parties	Airline Distance to Red Sulphur
600 miles	1	Massachusetts	0	0
550	2	Rhode Island	0	0
400-450	4	New York	2	350-400
200-350	2	Pennsylvania	2	350-400
0	0	Delaware	7	300
250	4	Maryland	5	250
200	2	Ohio	0	0
50-250	38	Virginia	28	50-250
0-50	6	West Virginia	47	0-150
100-250	6	North Carolina	1	200
250-350	15	South Carolina	1	300
350-400	6	Georgia	0	0
400-600	6	Alabama	2	400-600
400	1	Kentucky	0	0
0	0	Tennessee	2	200-550
0	0	Missouri	1	500
600	5	Mississippi	1	600
750	6	Louisiana	2	750

Table 3.3a Philadelphia to Warm Springs Trip of Peregrine Prolix in 1834
(Prolix, 1835, pp.9-18)

Day 1 6:00 a.m. Leave Philadelphia, move down Delaware River on boat 46 mi.
                    Follow Chesapeake & Delaware Canal across peninsula 14 mi
                    Change to paddle boat for trip down Chesapeake Bay 45 mi.
      3:30 p.m. Arrive Baltimore, board coach (soon to be replaced by railroad)
      9:30 p.m. Arrive Washington 40 mi.
Time elapsed, 15 ½ hrs. Average speed, 9.4 m.p.h. Daily travel, 145 mi.

Day 2 6:00 a.m. Leave Washington by omnibus, board Potomac River steamboat
                    Disembark at Potomac Creek, passing Mt. Vernon on way 55 mi.
                    Take coach to Fredericksburg, have dinner here 9 mi.
      3:00 p.m. Board coach to Orange Court House, have supper on the way
      9:30 p.m. Arrive at Orange 29 mi.
Time elapsed, 15 ½ hrs. Average speed, 6 m.p.h. Daily travel, 93 mi.

Day 3 5:00 a.m. Leave Orange on coach, stop for breakfast on the way
     11:00 a.m. Arrive Charlottesville (tour "Mr. Jefferson's University" option) 27 mi.
     12:00 a.m. Change coaches and cross Blue Ridge, enjoy splendid views
      7:00 p.m. Arrive Staunton, dining on the way (tour Weyer's Cave option) 32 mi.
Time elapsed, 14 hrs. Average speed, 4.2 m.p.h. Daily travel, 59 mi.

Day 4 4:00 a.m. Packed into coach and off to the Springs
      7:00 a.m. Arrive Fraziers for breakfast 14 mi.
      8:15 a.m. Leave by coach for Cloverdale, have dinner 19 mi.
      2:00 p.m. Leave for Warm Springs, grand views of the mountains on way
      7:00 p.m. Arrive Warm Springs 19 mi.
Time elapsed, 15 hrs. Average speed, 3.4 m.p.h. Daily travel, 52 mi

Grand total, 60 hrs. Grand total, 349 mi.

Note: The distance from Warm Springs to Red Sulphur Springs via White Sulphur and Salt Sulphur would be 81 miles. Most 19th century travelers would have stopped at each for a few days, as did Peregrine Prolix, but the actual travel time would be about twenty hours, so to travel directly would add at least two days to any trip. For these legs, Prolix found the stage coaches full, so had to hitch rides with travelers driving their own carriages.

Table 3.3b Warm Springs to Philadelphia Return Trip of Peregrine Prolix in 1834
(Prolix, 1835, pp.75-90)

Day 1   Warm Springs to Fraziers by same route as outbound trip
Time elapsed, 12 hrs.   Average speed, 3.2 m.p.h.   Daily travel, 38 mi.

Day 2	8:00 a.m.	Leave Fraziers by coach	
	12:00 a.m.	Arrive Harrisonburg for dinner	22 mi.
	2:00 p.m.	Leave for New Market along beautiful Shenandoah Valley	
	5:00 pm.	Arrive but no place to stay, so move on to next stop	20 mi.
	8:00 p.m.	Arrive Mt. Jackson	7 mi.

Time elapsed, 12 hrs.   Average speed, 4.1 m.p.h.   Daily travel, 49 mi.

Day 3	6:00 a.m.	Leave Mt. Jackson, take coach north along Shenandoah Valley	
	10:00 a.m.	Arrive Woodstock for breakfast	13 mi.
	11:00 a.m.	Leave for Winchester	
	5:00 p.m.	Arrive Taylor's Hotel	28 mi.

Time elapsed, 11 hrs.   Average Speed, 3.7 m.p.h.   Daily travel, 41 mi.

Day 4	7:30 a.m.	Leave Winchester, take coach again along Shenandoah Valley	
	2:30 p.m.	Arrive Harpers Ferry, have dinner, stay at Fitzsimmons Hotel	30 mi.
		Later enjoy stupendous scenery, visit arsenals and manufactories	

Time elapsed, 5 hrs.   Average speed, 6 m.p.h.   Daily travel, 30 mi.

Day 5	3:00 a.m.	"Routed" by canal boat captain, but got some sleep on boat	
	5:00 a.m.	Leave Harpers Ferry on Potomac River canal boat	
	8:30 a.m.	Arrive Point of Rocks, have breakfast	12 mi.
	9:00 a.m.	Leave for Baltimore on Railroad	
		(First half trip cars drawn by horses, second by steam!)	
	4:00 p.m.	Arrive Baltimore, stay at Fountain Inn	50 mi.

Time elapsed, 11 hrs.   Average speed, 5.7 m.p.h.   Daily travel, 62 mi.

Day 6   Baltimore to Philadelphia by same route as outbound trip
Time elapsed, 15 ½ hrs.   Average speed, 9.4 m.p.h.   Daily travel, 145 mi.

Grand total, 66 ½ hrs.   Grand total 365 mi.

The Financial Panic of 1837

The frequency of financial panics in the nineteenth century is shown in Appendix 1. According to Aliber and Kindleberger, 2015, p.20, "the cycle of manias and panics results from the supply of credit which increases rapidly in good times, and then when economic growth slackens, the rate of growth of credit declines sharply triggering the decline in the prices of currencies and securities." The panic of 1837 was one of the longest depressions in United States history, lasting about six years until 1843. Business in the South was affected by the collapse of cotton prices while the number of visitors to the Springs was cut in half. Two Spring owners had invested heavily in new buildings to accommodate the previous crowds and they were John B. Lewis, owner of Sweet Springs and William Burke. Now, Sweet Springs went on the auction block in 1852 (Gish, 2009, p.101) and Red Sulphur in 1843 (*Charleston Courier*, May 29, 1843). In the case of Sweet Springs, ownership was in the third generation of the Lewis family and the Gish book is devoted to the details. It is entitled "Sweet Springs: A Bittersweet Legacy" for good reasons; the closure was very sad. The beautiful classical brick structure still extant was designed and built by William B. Phillips, protégé of Thomas Jefferson.

Also sad was the fate of Red Sulphur. Burke had signed five Trust Deeds during the period 1834 to 1840 to build the much-admired resort in 1842 but was forced to give it all up to the principal creditors Andrew Beirne and James A. Dunlap. The auction occurred on August 17, 1843, but Dunlap was on his death bed, dying on August 19 so Beirne assumed half-ownership and the other half was shared by brothers Addison and Alexander Dunlap. From this point The Red was to last for nearly a century, during which modest changes were made; but Burke's buildings were there to be enjoyed by thousands of visitors over these years.

William Burke was philosophical about this and wrote about the fate of the Springs in view of the economy, "...they may and will be temporarily depressed by the universal declension of prosperity; but should that prosperity again revive, and the legislature prove alive to the true interests of the State, and connect the different springs with each other, and with the James River improvement, by fine macadamized roads, and extend those roads to the boundaries of Tennessee and southern Kentucky, and also to Guyandotte and Parkersburg, those Springs will not only become intrinsically of immense value, but it is difficult to estimate the increase of revenue and wealth which that portion of the State, now comparatively unprofitable, will produce. Many years will not have elapsed before England and France will annually send multitudes of invalids to those unrivalled fountains, and we shall see those beautiful valleys teeming with living beings from every quarter of the globe." (Burke, 1846, pp.10)

Burke's vision was a little over optimistic, but the turnpike system was in for a great expansion, together with advances in canals, railroads, and steamboats, as will be seen in the next chapter. But first, a final word from William Burke "If a solitary individual, whose eye may rest on these pages, shall chance to bless his labours, they will be amply compensated" (ibid, p.11)

Chapter 4

Transportation in the Mid-Nineteenth Century

"The decade of the 1830s in Virginia was one of the most fabled in its history. Everywhere, men were talking about turnpikes, canals, and railroads. The words 'speculation,' 'promise,' and 'opulence' punctuated the conversations of gentlemen capitalists who gathered in drawing rooms, taverns, and coffee houses. In the mountains, a rash of turnpikes replaced the bad roads that had once made the springs so inaccessible" (Gish, 2009, p.30).

This chapter is perhaps a *non sequitur* in the Springs chronology but is placed here simply because people traveled up to seven or eight hundred miles to get here, so some appreciation of the difficulties involved in mid-nineteenth century travel is needed at this point. Also, as the quotation above implies, great technological strides were being made in the transportation field (see Table 4.1). The general layout and operation of stagecoaches, steamboats, and canal packets will be discussed with some idea of the pros and cons of each, as gained from the contemporary accounts of our forebears.

For the "time traveler" out there, Figure 4.1 provides a list of available books for 1844 designed especially for folks planning a trip to the Springs. A number of these are currently available in reprint form, including Tanner's guides which give "Tables of Distances, by Stage, Canal, and Steamboat Routes." The original contains maps but unfortunately, the reprint does not.

Stagecoaches and Private Carriages

Stagecoaches had been around since colonial times, but by the 1830's, improvements in roadbuilding as well as in coach design made this form of transportation faster, as well as more comfortable. The stagecoach companies had gained the contract to carry the U.S. Mail in 1785 (Table 4.1), so this imposed a regularity in the scheduling, the "stage" part of the term refers to the fact that the coach stopped to change teams at livery stables or hotels about every 10 miles; that is, about every two hours. Also, "The 'post-horses' for the use of private carriages were obtained from the stage barns enroute, swapping them at the same places the stages did" (Reilly, 2020). The keeping of 'post-horses' for hire was one of the money-making accounts of the

BOOKS FOR TRAVELLERS.

LATELY RECEIVED, and for sale by F. TAYLOR: The Northern Traveller, a guide through the Middle and Northern States and the Canadas, 1 pocket volume.

Tanner's Tourist's Guide through the Central States, 1 small volume, with many maps, plans, &c.

The White Sulphur Papers, or Life at the Springs of Western Virginia, 1 vol.

The Mineral Springs of Western Virginia, by Wm. Burke, 1 vol.

The Fauquier Springs of Virginia, by a visiter, 1 volume.

The Salt Sulphur Springs of Virginia, by T. D. Mutter, M. D.

The Red Sulphur Springs of Virginia, by the late H. Huntt, M. D.

Tanner's Travelling Map of Virginia, Maryland, and Delaware, with the roads, canals, railroads, routes, distances, &c. &c.

Tanner's Canals, Railroads, &c. of the United States;

And many other Books of the same kind, too numerous for the limits of an advertisement.

F. TAYLOR,
Bookseller, near Gadsby's Hotel.

june 28—tf

Figure 4.1 These books attest to the popularity of the Virginia Springs for Travelers at the time, and most are still available in reprinted form. The Tanner's Guides are very comprehensive, although unfortunately the maps are not included in modern copies.
(*The Daily Madisonian*, DC, Jun 29, 1844).

stagecoach business, and there was always extra stock for this purpose. Ten cents per mile for a two-horse team was the usual price, and the charge was twenty-five cents for a four-horse complement" (Coleman, 1935, p.93).

The iconic stagecoach design was developed by two gentlemen in a small city in central New Hampshire, as described by Schreiber, 2011, p.4, "The prime achievement of Downing and Abbot was their development of the design that, by 1830 had been perfected as the 'Concord coach.' In the early nineteenth century, coach design had shifted away from the traditional box shape toward oval body design. The rounded top was of little utilitarian value, however, for as long-haul travel became more common, transport of passengers' baggage became difficult. This problem was alleviated only partially by employment of 'boots' (leather-covered baggage trunks located under the driver's seat or at the rear). Abbot and Downing built their carriages, from the beginning, with flat tops and rounded bottoms, a shape which in the early 1830s was becoming standard in the American industry. What distinguished the Concord coach uniquely was its suspension system. Unlike other manufacturers, who used metal spring-type suspensions, Abbot and Downing employed 'thoroughbraces.' These were strips of leather riveted together to a thickness of about three inches, attached to run lengthwise, and upon which the coach body was suspended. The thoroughbrace gave the vehicle a swinging motion, instead of the harsher up-and-down motion produced by the conventional spring motions. The Concord coach was, as Mark Twain described it, 'an imposing cradle on wheels.'"

"Still more important, the Concord coach was built well. Stout oak was used for the frame and body. Its wheels were cut of ash, then hand fitted to rims and hubs. Although each coach was finished and decorated according to the purchaser's specifications, most were painted ornately, with yellow running gear and red bodies, decorated with emblems or figures. The interiors were a veritable 'Aladdin's cave' of fine leather, polished metal, and wood paneling. Whether simple or ornate, an Abbot and Downing vehicle was built to earn the reputation that it don't break down, but only wears out" (ibid., p.4). This reference shows vintage paintings of trains leaving the factory for points west loaded with thirty stagecoaches at a time.

Stagecoach travel had its pros and cons as pointed out by Coleman (1935, p.91); "A traveler in the stage-coach days was not tantalized by the fleeting half glimpse of the places as in railroad or automobile travel today. He had ample time to view any unusual, beautiful, or historic spot, as he passed. He had leisure to make inquiry, he had many hours to hear his fellow traveler's tale, or that of the driver. This pictures the romantic side of stage-coach travel in central Kentucky. The prosaic side attracts attention when we look at the schedules of some of the lines, which invariably announce departures at three, four, or five A.M.—all before daylight. It mattered little how long was your journey, or where you were going, your coach always started before daylight. You had to arise in the dark, dress in a room most feebly illuminated, eat a hurriedly prepared breakfast, and start out in the blackness of the night or depressing chill of early morning."

Johnson (2019, p.131) quotes a West Virginia rider concerning stagecoach travel, "If any old timer tells you about the pleasures of a trip on the stage, don't believe him, as you can't pack that amount of discomfort in the same length of time any other way. When the roads were on the level you traveled in a cloud of dust, and when you were on the hills, there was more rocks in the road then you could count, and the driver hit every one of them. There were three seats, the front and rear ones had firm backs, and the people in the middle seat had to depend on a broad strap of leather fastened to the sides of the coach, and while all were more or less scrambled, the ones on the middle seat were double scrambled."

With this level of discomfort, one did not want to travel all night, although the mail had to go through, and the stagecoaches were obliged to maintain round-the-clock schedules. However, staying in a coaching inn could also be rough. "While special rooms might be set aside for genteel travelers to enjoy, a traveler

Table 4.1 Key Developments in Transportation, 1783-1883

1783. The first wagon road was opened from Warm Springs through the Allegheny Mountains to Lewisburg (Stuart, 1798 in Shuck, 1992, p.49).

1785. Stagecoach companies gained the contract, previously held by post riders, to carry the U.S. Mail (Johnson, 2019, p.22).

1807. Fulton's steamboat went from New York to Albany at 5 mph (Srinivasan, 2017, p.62-3).

1816. Mississippi River Steamboat design was standardized (Gillespie, 2011, p.11).

1817. The Turnpike Act of Virginia became law and allowed the state to share costs with both investors and users (Martindale, 2017, p.4).

1823. The macadam road surface, developed in Scotland, was introduced in North America, and the first example extended from Hagerstown, MD southeastward.

1827. The iconic Concord Stagecoach design was standardized by Abbott-Downing, NH (Schreiber, 2011, p.4).

1827. The Lewisburg to Charleston, WV stage line went into operation (Johnson, 2019, p.146).

1828. The Baltimore & Ohio Railroad broke ground for tracks, with horses used initially to pull the trains (Srinivasan, 2017, p.81-2).

1831. The White Sulphur & Sweet Springs Turnpike was chartered (Martindale, 2017, Table 6).

1833. Concord Coaches were running over Kentucky routes (Coleman, 1935, p.51).

1834. The Valley Turnpike was built from Winchester to Harrisonburg, VA. It was continued to Staunton to Winchester, a total of 115 miles and macadamized by 1840, (Johnson, 2019, p.145).

1835. The first turnpike in Kentucky was from Maysville to Lexington (Coleman, 1935, p.233).

1840. The 146-mile James River Canal, Richmond to Lynchburg was completed (Shaw, 1990, p.114).

1845. Most western springs turnpikes were completed (Burke, 1846, p.324).

1850. A network of macadamized roads was finished in Kentucky, having taken 15 years to build (Coleman, 1935, p.233).

1856. The Norfolk & Western Railroad was completed through Newbern, now Dublin, VA, 38 miles from Red Sulphur Springs (Reger and Price, 1926, p.12).

1873. The Chesapeake & Ohio Railroad was completed through Hinton and came within 12 miles of Red Sulphur Springs at Talcott (Reger and Price, 1926, p.8-10).

1883. The Norfolk & Western Railroad was extended through Lurich in adjacent Mercer County, 11 miles and a ferry ride from Red Sulphur Springs (Reger and Price, 1926, p.13).

with lighter pockets might find himself snug in a bed with several other passengers, side by side, or perhaps enjoying a pallet of straw of uncertain age upon the bedroom floor" (Johnson, 2019, p.75).

Improvements of the road system were obviously needed and the Turnpike Act of Virginia was signed in 1817. This led to the completion of a network by 1845. These turnpikes connected the springs and were supported financially by the Springs owners (Table 4.1, Figure 4.2). "This Act required all roads to be at least sixty feet wide with eighteen feet well covered with gravel or stone, and at all times kept firm and smooth, free from all mud holes, ruts and other obstructions, and in all respects fit for the use of heavy laden wagons, and of other carriages in dry weather, between the first of May, and the thirty-first day of October, and fit for the use of horses and foot travelers at all times" (Martindale, 2017, p.4).

Another improvement was the introduction of the macadam road surface which set a limit to the size and weight of the stones used in paving the road surface, the weight being six ounces. "With the coming of the "metaled" or hard-surfaced roads, the stagecoaches profited greatly, increasing the average speeds from three and four miles an hour, to seven or eight, counting time lost for stoppages" (Coleman, 1935, p.235).

In summary, stagecoach travel improved gradually during the 1800s but was never replaced completely by boat or train; for instance, by 1890 you could get from Washington D.C. to Lowell, WV, in nine hours by rail, but it took another three hours to travel the twelve miles by stage to Red Sulphur. So the long trips by stage may have been over but it was still needed as a feeder for motorized vehicles, and this was true into the early twentieth century.

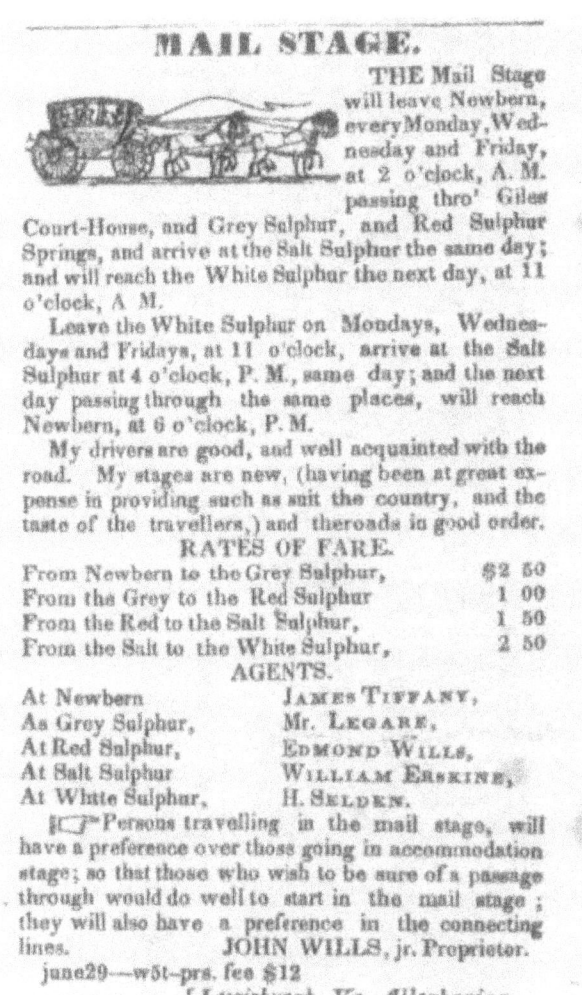

Figure 4.2
This is the stagecoach schedule in the Virginia Springs areas complete with rates of fare and names of agents.
(*The National Register and National Whig*, TN, Aug 8, 1836)

Figure 4.3 The top panel is for travel westward by canal boat from Richmond and the bottom for travel northeastward by estuary steamer. Note that "packet" meant that it carried passengers as well as freight.
(*Richmond Enquirer*, Oct 31, 1845)

Figure 4.4 This is Rapid Transit, nineteenth century style, and was designed especially for the springs trade.
(*The Baltimore Sun*, Jun 18, 1881)

Steamboats on the Big Rivers

"Western River Steamboats were built to run in shallow depths and in narrow confines on waterways devoid of swells. They carried freight by the hundreds of tons and passengers by the score. They were propelled by paddlewheels, and they literally could lift themselves over shoals and reefs" (Gillespie, 2001, p. xiii). The passengers traveled on the second deck, termed the 'boiler deck' and "It consisted of a long interior room known as the main cabin or saloon. Initially, this cabin served as both sleeping quarters and social hall, with berths cordoned off by curtains. The after-section was the 'ladies' cabin,' which was delineated by a partition. Male passengers were accommodated in the forward main cabin, where one would also find a bar, a barbershop, and the offices of the clerk and steward. By the 1840s the curtained berths of the main cabin had given way to private staterooms that now lined either side of the cabin. Staterooms featured two berths, and were further adorned with etched-glass windows, curtains, mosquito-bars (netting), toilet stands, drawers, chairs, carpets, and all the elegant necessaries of a cozy bedroom" (ibid., p.17).

This general design was standardized in 1816 and seems elegant and efficient in comparison with the stagecoach. However, some of the disadvantages pointed out by Gillespie include the fact that the boat had to stop twice a day to get "wooded up" with fuel, and since the money was in the cargo, some days were wasted waiting for a load to show up on the pier. "These smoking, puffing works of carpenter gothic usually wore themselves out or sank to the bottom within five years of their launching. The prospect of suddenly being hurled skyward in a horrific boiler explosion or washed into icy waters from the deck of a sinking packet loomed as very real possibilities for the average steamboat passengers. The explosion and fire that killed 1,547 passengers and crew onboard the steamboat *Sultana* on April 26, 1865, remains to this day the deadliest transportation catastrophe in United States history" (Ibid. p. xiv).

The Mississippi-Ohio River system was of course the one useful for the Springs trade. The Great Kanawha, which is the lower 97 miles of the New River, is navigable, however, it trends in a north-south direction, so trade seems was mainly with the upstream course of the Ohio (Sutphin & Andre, 1991, pp. 2, 53). Stagecoach advertisements connect Charleston, WV, with the Ohio River trade at Guyandotte (now Huntington) and this cuts off two legs of a triangle in the two rivers. One 1844 stagecoach advertisement following this route would get the passenger from Charleston to Cincinnati in 35 hours, travelling overland by day and along the river at night (ibid., p.20).

So the steamboat age deserves its romantic image, but it was all over in about 60 years, that is, in the 1870s, outcompeted by the railroad (Gillespie, 2001, p.275). This is because the railroad cut a straight swath across the midcontinent while the rivers had constant meanders, often superimposed on major changes in direction. And of course, the trains could travel at a much faster rate of speed, once they were pulled by steam engines as opposed to horses.

Canal Packets

The most useful canal from the point of view of the springs trade was the James River system. It began in the east with the estuary of the lower James River branching from Chesapeake Bay near Norfolk and extended about 80 miles northwest to Richmond (Figure 4.3). The westerly canal portion was surveyed as early as 1786, and by 1816 navigation of a "rapid-shooting, rock-dodging sort was possible." However, completion of the 146-mile canal from Richmond to Lynchburg took until 1840, and the remainder through the Blue Ridge to Buchanan, another 50 miles, took until 1851. On completion it had 90 locks, 23 feeder dams, and 12 aqueducts. So the construction of canals was much more involved than that of roads or railroads, and by 1854 serious competition with the railroads had begun (Kirkwood, 1963, pp.7-18; Shaw, 1990, pp.112-116).

A "packet" was a vessel that carried passengers as well as freight and was about 75 feet long and 11 feet wide. Kirkwood (ibid., p.26) includes the following description, "those used in the East were all of similar design. Right in the bow, carefully set off from the rest of the boat, was a tiny cuddy for the crew. Next back of this came the ladies' dressing room, sometimes cut off from the main cabin only by a red curtain. Next was the main cabin, 36 to 45 feet long, which was a saloon and dining room by day and men's dormitory by night. Back of this was the bar, and finally, at the very stern, was the kitchen, almost always presided over by a negro cook, who was usually the bartender also. He was kept busy fifteen to eighteen hours per day."

A journey on the canal is an experience to be treasured in memory, as one passenger remembered. "To sit all day upon the deck of the long, low boat, luxuriously at ease, while the mules trot cheerfully along the towpath, drawing the staunch craft upon the waveless water, between the narrow banks, and the horn of the driver, from time to time sends forth the mournful note of signal for the locks, while the superb scenery, which all along the route is unfolded to view, was an enjoyment without the tantalizing fleetness that characterizes travel by steam or electricity. What an absorbing interest there was when the locks were raised and the keeper came out and filled, or let out, the water, according as the boat was ascending of descending the river, and opened or shut the ponderous gates, and one experienced the queer sensations of slowly rising or falling with the water!" (ibid, p.26).

Kirkwood also described the cons of canal travel. "It was the accommodations for the night that were not conducive to pleasure. The main cabin necessarily had to serve as both the dining and sleeping quarters and in the space designed for 30 or 40 people, whatever number happened to be on board, were packed in. Usually only a curtain divided the quarters for women and children from those of men. About 9 o'clock, the boat hands put in place the three-tiered berths and slung them by ropes or leather straps from the ceiling. The berths were very narrow and short and furnished with a lumpy mattress and pillow. An overflow crowd, for whom there were no berths, received a mattress and had to sleep on the dining room tables or on the cabin floor" (ibid. p.27).

In conclusion, canal travel was fine for folks who had access to one that trended in the right direction; and in this respect it was similar to river boat travel without some of the hazards. The dream of George Washington for a navigation system traversing the Appalachian Mountains from east to west was never completed and soon the railroad surged ahead (Figure 4.4), using the very same valleys of the James, New and Kanawha Rivers to get to the Ohio River Valley.

A Statistical Comparison of the Different Travel Modes

Table 4.2a,b compares several examples of travel on roads, rivers, and canals, and one example of a trip combining all three. For these to be useful, on-the-ground mileage plus elapsed travel time are needed, so detailed diaries, published schedules, or race results contain the best data, though difficult to find. The travel distance (Column A) was chosen to be as long as possible, but stagecoach routes are naturally the shortest and river boat routes the longest. The airline, or straight-line distance (B) is the straightest with stagecoaches, and the longest with rivers which have both short wave-length meanders and major changes of course. The travel time (C) includes stops for stages to change horses, steamboats to refuel, and canal boats to go through locks. The total time column (D) is just for stagecoaches and includes both dinners and hotel sleepovers. The ground speed (A/C) is the calculated miles per hour, and steamboats were fastest with an average of 11.7 mph, stages second at 5.5 mph, and canals slowest at 4.7 mph. The actual speed (B/D) uses the straight-line distance and is more even with steamboats at 5.5 mph, stages at 4.5 mph, and canal boats at 3.5 mph. Finally, the route efficiency (B x 100/A) shows the roads to be by far the most direct and the rivers and canals the least direct.

In summary, travel was about one-tenth the rate of ground travel today, and the railroad was outcompeting its contemporaries along many corridors by the mid-nineteenth century. As has been mentioned, the stagecoach system remained as a feeder for the others into the twentieth century—and it was the only public transportation in outlying districts. Planning a seven- or eight-hundred mile trip to the springs must have been a daunting task and a tedious one at that—best to take a steamboat and enjoy the experience!

Table 4.2a - Statistics for Different Travel Modes

No.	Conveyance Used	Start-Finish	Date	Reference
1	Stagecoach	Charleston-White Sulphur Spr. WV	1870	Johnson, 2019, pp.130-1
	same	vice versa	1870	ibidem
2	Stagecoach	Sweet Springs-Hot Springs VA	1834	Prolix, 1836, p.66
3	Stagecoach	Maysville-Lexington KY	1838	Coleman, 1935 p.233
4	same	Covington- Lexington KY	?	ibidem, p.219
5	Canal Boat	Richmond-Lynchburg VA	1840	Kirkwood, 1963, pp.24, 29
	same	vice versa	1840	ibidem
6	Canal Boat	Albany-Buffalo NY	1835	Shaw, 1990, p.48
7	same	same	1835	ibidem
8	Canal Boat	Toledo OH-Lafayette IN	1834	Shaw, 1990, p. 155
9	Steamboat	Marietta OH-St. Louis MO	1833	Gillespie, 2001, pp.150-5
10	Steamboat	New Orleans LA-Louisville KY	1853	Gillespie, 2001, pp.184-5
	same	same	1853	ibidem
11	Steamboat	New Orleans LA-St. Louis MO	1870	Gillespie, 2001 pp. 188-207
	same	same	1870	ibidem
12	Ocean Steamer	Charleston SC-New York City	1838	John Hinton Diary
13	Mixed	Philadelphia-Warm Springs VA	1834	Prolix, 1836, pp.9-18
	same	vice versa	1834	Prolix, 1836, pp.75-90

Table 4.2b - Statistics for Different Travel Modes

No.	Travel Distance A	Airline Distance B	Travel Time C	Total Time D	Ground Speed A/C	Actual Speed B/D	Route Efficiency Bx100/A	Comments
1	110 mi	84 mi	34 hrs	34 hrs	3.2 mph	2.5 mph	76%	Mountainous
	110 mi	84 mi	36 hrs	36 hrs	3.1 mph	2.3 mph	76%	Return trip
2	38 mi	33.5 mi	6.5 hrs	8 hrs	5.8 mph	4.2 mph	88%	Mountainous
3	64 mi	57 mi	8 hrs	8 hrs	8 mph	7.1 mph	89%	Level ground
4	82 mi	70 mi	11 hrs	11 hrs	7.5 mph	6.4 mph	85%	same
5	146 mi	100 mi	33 hrs	33 hrs	4.4 mph	3.0 mph	68%	Up current
	146 mi	100 mi	31.5 hrs	31.5 hrs	4.6 mph	3.2 mph	68%	Down current
6	363 mi	265 mi	120 hrs	120 hrs	3 mph	2.2 mph	73%	Average Packet
7	363 mi	265 mi	50 hrs	50 hrs	7.3 mph	5.3 mph	73%	Fast Packet
8	242 mi	200 mi	56 hrs	56 hrs	4.3 mph	3.6 mph	83%	Scheduled Packet
9	1095 mi	460 mi	174 hrs	220 hrs	6.3 mph	2.1 mph	42%	Downstream
10	1440 mi	650 mi	105.5 hrs	105.5 hrs	13.6 mph	6.2 mph	45%	Race winner
	1440 mi	650 mi	106.4 hrs	106.4 hrs	13.5 mph	6.1 mph	45%	Race looser
11	1200 mi	620 mi	91.5 hrs	91.5 hrs	13.1 mph	6.7 mph	52%	Race winner
	1200 mi	620 mi	98 hrs	98 hrs	12.2 mph	6.3 mph	52%	Race looser
12	700 mi	650 mi	120 hrs	120 hrs	5.8 mph	5.4 mph	93%	Down current
13	349 mi	280 mi	60 hrs	85 hrs	5.7 mph	3.3 mph	80%	Mixed terrain
	366 mi	280 mi	66.5 hrs	80 hrs	5.5 mph	3.5 mph	76%	Return diff. route

Red Sulphur Springs, West Virginia

Chapter 5

The Owner Families: Beirne, Dunlap, and Campbell 1843-1861

The antebellum ownership of the Red Sulphur Springs shifted to a succession of prominent local families who, for the most part, invested in, and maintained the resort but seemingly did not develop it further. Indeed, the economy had recovered and the Springs in general flourished until the Civil War, although visitor records for The Red are lacking for this time. Altogether, the three families generated seven owners, and of these, four died prematurely. The resulting complex legal background is outlined in Table 5.1 and the following section is devoted to brief biographies of the owners, including any hands-on involvement with The Red each may have had. Information has been gleaned from Morton (1916), and legal references are listed in Table 5.1.

Andrew Beirne, Sr. (1771-1845) emigrated from Ireland in 1793 and married a local girl, Eleanor Grey Keenan in 1800. He opened a store with brother George in the new town and county of Union and Monroe. In addition to being very successful in the mercantile area, he was a great landowner and developed Walnut Grove, an estate of 2200 acres of prime farmland, just northwest of Union. By the time of his death, he also owned plantations in Alabama and Mississippi. His involvement with Red Sulphur Springs was to lend money to Wm. Burke during the time of his great building spree in the 1830's. He inherited a half interest in the resort in the auction of 1843 for this support although apparently he was not involved in running it; indeed, he was busy as a Virginia State Senator and then a U.S. Congressman during much of this time.

Oliver Beirne (1811-1888) was the son of Andrew and Eleanor, married Margaret Melinda Caperton, a member of a prominent Union family in 1831. Early in his career, Oliver made a great deal of money buying and selling in the sugarcane business, being based in New York while working with a partner in New Orleans named John Burnsides. He was selected as executor of his father's estate which he divided among seven siblings in equal amounts valued at $75,000, including property, money, and slaves. Interestingly, the Red Sulphur property was not included, so Oliver, as executor, was the de facto owner from 1843 to 1855 when he decided to auction it off and divide the proceeds among the interested parties. He seems not to have involved himself in the operation of The Red during this long interval, perhaps because he was fully occupied with other pursuits; This included the management of the Sweet Springs resort, which he became

Table 5.1, Ownership Changes and Legal Records, 1843-1861

Nov. 1843. Andrew Beirne Sr. & James A. Dunlap had loaned money to Wm. Burke for his building binge in the 1830's, but Burke defaulted, and Dunlap died just before the auction, so the Red Sulphur Springs was auctioned off. In the auction, Beirne acquired half ownership while James' executors, his brothers Addison & Alexander Dunlap each acquired a quarter share (Deed Book O., p.31-47, and p.86).

Mar 1845. Andrew Beirne died, and in the Deed of Partition, each of his seven children received a share of property, slaves, money, etc. valued at $75,000 (Deed Book, p., p.11). However, Red Sulphur Springs was not mentioned, and partial ownership appears to have remained within the Beirne family for the next 10 years through the auspices of executor Oliver, Beirne's son.

Mar 1853. Alexander Dunlap died, and his will stated that his share in Red Sulphur was to remain as it was until a favorable opportunity for selling occurred (Will Book., 5, p.523).

Oct 1854. Oliver Beirne filed a bill as plaintiff against the other owners of Red Sulphur, including four of his siblings, the executors of Alexander Dunlap, and also Addison Dunlap, and Mary Ann Dunlap, widow of Alexander, arguing that the property could not be divided and that it was in the interest of the parties to auction the resort as a unit (Chancery Order Book 1, p.196).

Jul 1855. The Circuit Court of Monroe County advertised "Red Sulphur Springs for Sale" in six newspapers (Newspapers.com, *Richmond Enquirer*, Jul 31, 1855).

Oct 1855. The Circuit Court announced that the Springs had been sold to Addison Dunlap for $29,500 and that the proceeds had been divided as follows; one half to Oliver & George Beirne, executors of Andrew Beirne, deceased, one fourth to Alexander Haynes & Richard Shanklin, executors of Alexander Dunlap, and one fourth to Addison Dunlap (Chancery Order Book 1, p.322).

Jun 1856. It was announced in a Red Sulphur Springs advertisement, "The dining room will be under the supervision of Maj. Thomas S. Campbell, one of the new proprietors." (Newspapers.com, *Charleston Mercury*, SC, Jun 25, p.3).

Feb 1858. "R.V. Shanklin, executor of Alexander Dunlap "...sold to Thomas S. Campbell a one-third interest in the Red Sulphur Springs property..." for $12,502.49 and "Addison Dunlap, Thomas S. Campbell, and brother Isaac H. Campbell entered into a partnership for the purpose of carrying on business at Red Sulphur Springs." (Dunlap versus Shanklin, *Court of Appeals, WV, West Virginia Reports*, 1877, pp.663, 665).

Nov 1859. The Campbell's purchase price of Red Sulphur (see above) fell short for complicated reasons, but the details were not sorted out until after the death of the Campbell brothers, so this had no apparent effect on the operation of the Springs (Dunlap versus Shanklin, ibid. p.664).

Sep 1860. Thomas S. Campbell died and then Isaac H. Campbell died in Oct of 1861.

joint owner about 1852. Also, his brother Andrew, Jr. was indebted to him for $50,000 in 1855, so the sale of The Red would generate the needed cash. According to Morton, Oliver had a great capacity for business organization, and he died with a net worth of about six million dollars.

James Alexander Dunlap (1799-1843) was the son of Alexander Dunlap, Sr. and Jane Alexander Dunlap, a founding family of Union, and married Francis Catherine McElhenny in 1830. It has been said of the Dunlap family, "In the public life of Monroe and in professional and business careers, the members of this connection have been conspicuous" (Morton, 1916 p.337). James was a partner with Andrew Beirne, Sr., in the trust deeds to support the William Burke expansion projects at the Red. In 1838 he bought a 675-acre farm on lower Hans Creek. This farm is a little over four miles from Red Sulphur Springs, that is known to this day as the Dunlap Farm. James had loaned money to Wm. Burke in the 1830's and then was hired by Burke to run Red Sulphur in the waning days of his ownership in 1841-42 (Monroe County Deed Book N, p.59), but he never became an owner because he died just two days before The Red went on the auction block. He is included here because he was in line for ownership and appointed his brothers Addison and Alexander as executors and left his plantation on Hans Creek to the two of them.

Addison Dunlap (1804-1871), brother of James, married English immigrant Elizabeth Clara Petrie in 1834. He acted as partner with brother Alexander, Jr. (1812-1853), who married Mary Ann Shanklin in 1838. They each bought one-quarter share of Red Sulphur Springs at the auction of 1843. As for the Hans Creek house, there are records that Addison moved there in 1848 (Deed Book P, p.490) and Alexander may have lived there in the interim. About this time, Alexander opened a store at Red Sulphur and a ledger representing the years 1849-51 is the subject of the next section of this chapter. Alexander bought a house on Indian Creek about a mile downstream from the resort in 1849 (Monroe County Deed Book P, p.550) which he occupied until dying prematurely in 1853. This house survives as the Dunlap House on Indian Creek. Addison was less active at The Red than Alexander, but he did become the president of the Red & Blue Sulphur Springs Turnpike (Martindale, 2017, p.50) which was designed to complete the turnpike circuit of the resorts in Monroe and Greenbrier Counties. In the Census of 1850, Addison is listed as a farmer and records show that he supplied eggs and bacon for sale at Alexander's store.

Thomas S. Campbell (1806-1860), grandson of Samuel and Elizabeth, early settlers of Red Sulphur Springs, was unmarried, while his brother and partner, Isaac Henry Campbell (1808-1861) was married to Nancy A. Vass in 1835. Prior to their involvement with the resort, these brothers were joint owners of an 800-acre farm, now known as Crumps Bottom, along the New River adjacent to Red Sulphur Springs. The farm yielded up to 75 bushels of corn per acre which in turn would fatten 200 head of hogs and 100 head of cattle each year, according to Isaac's son, Lewis P. Campbell (see Appendix Five). After the sale of Red Sulphur in 1855, Addison Dunlap brought in the brothers as partners; however, Thomas was the one to play a direct role at the resort in the form of supervisor of the dining room in 1856. For some reason, the actual ownership sale was delayed until 1858, and by 1861 both brothers had died. From this point, Addison Dunlap was to carry on as owner, together with various heirs through the war years and beyond.

The question arises, if so few of these owners had a direct involvement in running the resort, then who did? It seems that the managing was done by hired hands and we find their names in advertisements or letters to the editor. Thus, the *Richmond Enquirer* (July 12, 1844) reported that "King, formerly of the White Sulphur is the present manager of The Red." Also, in 1859, Mr. G.H. Cowles was assigned entire control of the management. Interestingly, Cowles had been a patient at the resort in 1854-55 and took up residence "because I could not have any health anywhere else" (Burke, 1860, pp. 5 & 16). So, our knowledge is spotty, and sometimes they are even listed in newspaper articles as owners.

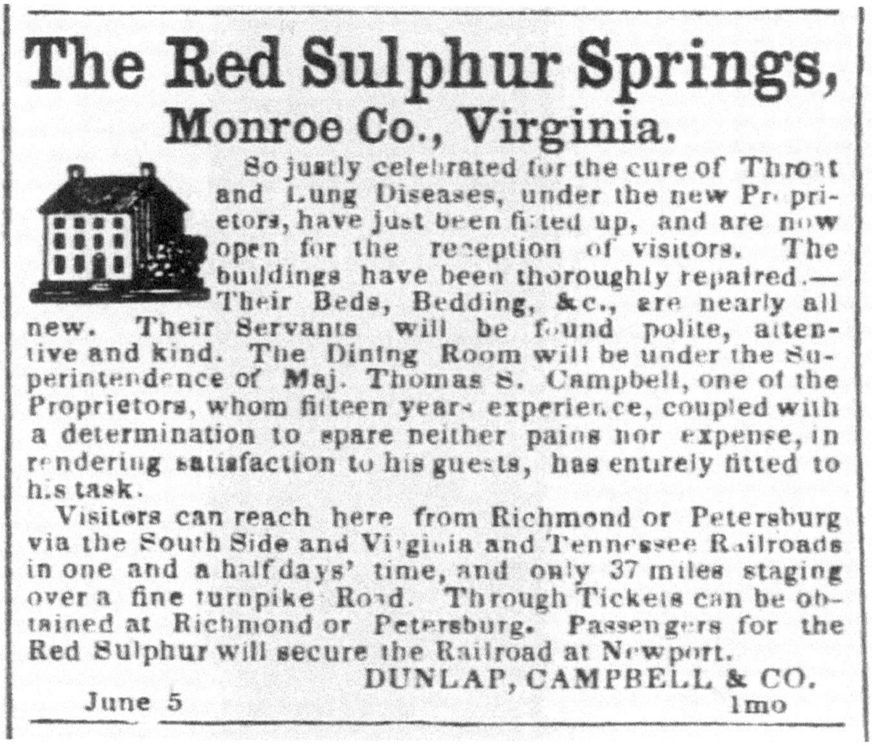

The Red Sulphur Springs,
Monroe Co., Virginia.

So justly celebrated for the cure of Throat and Lung Diseases, under the new Proprietors, have just been fitted up, and are now open for the reception of visitors. The buildings have been thoroughly repaired.—Their Beds, Bedding, &c., are nearly all new. Their Servants will be found polite, attentive and kind. The Dining Room will be under the Superintendence of Maj. Thomas S. Campbell, one of the Proprietors, whom fifteen years experience, coupled with a determination to spare neither pains nor expense, in rendering satisfaction to his guests, has entirely fitted to his task.

Visitors can reach here from Richmond or Petersburg via the South Side and Virginia and Tennessee Railroads in one and a half days' time, and only 37 miles staging over a fine turnpike Road. Through Tickets can be obtained at Richmond or Petersburg. Passengers for the Red Sulphur will secure the Railroad at Newport.

DUNLAP, CAMPBELL & CO.

June 5   1mo

Figure 5.1 This is another Red Sulphur Springs advertisement. It mentions that Major Thomas S. Campbell, one of the owners, also served as cook. (*The Charleston, SC, Mercury*, Jun 26, 1856).

The Alexander Dunlap Store of 1850

This article is based on a ledger in the archives of the Monroe County Historical Society (A. Dunlap, 1849-1851). It allows us to examine the range of products in a general country store in the middle nineteenth century. The first question to be addressed is which brother was A. Dunlap, the name on the ledger? Was it Addison or his younger brother, Alexander? The 1850 census lists Addison (1804-1871) as a farmer while Alexander (1812-1853) was the merchant in the family (Perkins, 1988). Since Addison was the census taker this attests to the accuracy of the family entries! Also, the store is mentioned in Alexander's will as being at the crossroads in Red Sulphur Springs; that is the point where Fitz Run enters Indian Creek, about where the modern State Route 12 crosses this creek. Alexander lived a mile downstream with his family of six, together with three others: two tailers and a physician. It is assumed that these worked at the store because two of the merchants were nephews, and included in the store were sewing materials, while doctors were in demand because the Red Sulphur Springs resort was a health spa. The 1850 census further lists in the next entry, the A. Dunlap & Co. as a Hotel, so that the store was probably on the ground floor while the rest of the building was for guests. Significantly, the Dunlap family was prominent in the politics of early Monroe County as well as in the financing and operation of the Red Sulphur Springs resort.

The layout of the ledger is a standard accounting format with the item name, quantity, and price of the product sold, and with the names of the debtors, and occasional creditor. For this article, eight days of sales, June 1 to June 8, 1850, were compiled in Tables 5.2a and b, with product name, number of sales, and price; and Table 5.3, provides the buyer's names, number of visits, and profession as listed in the Census. It should be mentioned that ledgers like this likely contained only those who bought on credit, and outsiders number just four out of 62 shoppers altogether. So there is probably bias in the products listed herein simply because the visitors' interests would have differed and buying on credit would not generally have been an option. The "visitor" names contrast with the census names, these customers were probably in the area as guests at the resort. There are question marks in the table where the surname matched the census entry but the given name was ambiguous and some of these could have been visitors; still, the number would have been small.

Questions to be addressed in this section are: what type of store was A. Dunlap & Co., where did the products come from, and what was the nature of the few items with names that may be unfamiliar to modern readers? Categories in Table 5.2a are devoted mostly to cloth, sewing, or ready-made clothes. Many of the yard goods were originally manufactured abroad and bear the names of countries like Ireland, Switzerland, and Holland, or of cities in foreign countries like Jeans (Genoa), Calico (Calcutta), or Jaconet (Jagannath, India) (Lederer, 1985). On the other hand, products like Domestic and some Linens were manufactured or hand woven locally and this included Check which was a linen weave. Interestingly, French Huguenots brought the culture and manufacture of linen to Ireland in the 17th century (Leyburn, 1962, p.128) and then continued their western trek to Virginia with the Scotch-Irish in the following century. The predominance of yard goods in Table 5.2a attests to the fact that most clothing was made at home but some, like the Coat, Pants & Vest combination, must have been made by the tailers employed by the store. This suit was bought by Alexander Dunlap, the store owner, and was the most expensive item sold during the week, while calico and domestic cloths were the cheapest fabrics and the most in demand. Also of interest is the hat category and the fact that Chip Hats dominate the rest in number of sales; in fact, most buyers bought two. A Chip Hat has been defined as a hat or bonnet woven of thin strips of wood or palm fiber and had been around since colonial times (Lederer, ibid.). It was probably made locally and was very inexpensive. Among the kitchen items, many were made of tin, including the candle mold and probably the coffee pot, so these could have been produced locally as well.

Table 5.2b begins with Patent Medicines, which were popular at the time and must have been bought by tourists at the Red Sulphur Springs as well (Wikipedia). The Vermifuge was to get rid of worms which were a problem with children in the area, while both Castor Oil and Epsom Salts were used as purgatives and were also popular at the time. Sanative is defined as conducive to physical and spiritual health so it was a general term and Bateman's Pectoral Drops were for disorders of the chest and included an opium solution. Jayne's Pills came in a variety of types for various complaints, including some of the ones listed above, so there is probably some duplication in the list. The thermometer was bought by a doctor and so it was placed in the Medical category. Under Household Articles, the binding of Graham's Magazine stands out. It was known for publishing short stories, such as Edgar Allan Poe's work, as well as critical reviews, articles on music, and information on fashion. It was ordered by Wm. Haynes, Dunlap's nephew and a salesman in his store. The Saddle-Making Supplies category was created for James Prentice who bought these items and was identified as a Saddler (Table 5.3). Finally, Services Provided includes the rental of oxen paid for by Samuel Phillips, a brick layer, who must have been working in the area because he visited the store seven times in one week.

The Dunlap Store was probably like many others at the time in terms of the range of products sold. Even Mathew's Trading Post near Lewisburg in the 1770's carried a similar range of categories, and many of the same items but with the addition of gun related supplies are an exception (Ziegler, 2019, p.133). Although the Dunlap Store was adjacent to a tourist venue, it still seems to have catered to the local inhabitants by providing some of the produce, such as butter, eggs, bacon, and sheep grown locally by farmers like Addison Dunlap of the neighboring Hans Creek valley. Most local residents must have grown and consumed their own produce and that would be the reason a wider range was not offered in the store. The exceptions would be coffee and tea of course. As for other imported items, they were hauled in from Lynchburg as the ledger shows that Benjamin M. Dunlap and Bartet Pack were paid $70.56 and $19.38, respectively, for these services during the period observed. These items would have been shipped up the James River Estuary to Richmond, about 100 miles, and then transported by canal to Lynchburg, 146 miles, where they would be picked up (Kirkwood, 1963). Early railroads were being built at that time but did not reach the Springs area of West Virginia until the 1870's. (This section of the book was initially published in the 2021 *Journal of the Greenbrier Historical Society*.)

Table 5.2a - Product Sales List - Part 1

Category/Product	Sales	Price	Category/Product	Sales	Price
Yard Goods (Cloth)			**Hats**		
Calico	10	$0.10-16 1/2 yd	Chip Hat	17	$0.20-0.25
Domestic (brown, black)	7	$0.10-0.12 1/2 yd	Fine Brand Bonnet	2	$2.50
Linen (low, brown, Irish)	6	$0.16 1/2-0.75 yd	Mexican Hat	1	$2.25
Jean	3	$0.33-0.45 yd	Fine Hat	1	$2.00
Gingham	1	$0.20 yd	Cashmere Hat	1	$1.00
Silk	1	$0.05 ?	Slouch Hat	2	$0.75
Alpaca	1	$0.75 yd	Child's Hat	1	$0.38
Check	1	$0.20 yd	Wool Hat	1	$0.25?
Wool	1	$0.28 yd			
Crepe	1	$0.75 yd			
Switz (Swiss?)	1	$0.62 yd	**Shoes**		
Holland	1	$0.72 yd	Best Shoes	3	$2.00
Bobinet	1	$0.38 yd	Best Brogans	1	$1.75
Jaconet	1	$0.34 yd	Coarse Shoes	1	$1.13
Lace	1	$0.12 yd	Shoes	1	$1.00
Ribbon	3	$0.13-0.25 yd	Misses Shoes	1	$0.50
			Black for Shoes	1	$0.50
Sewing Related					
Indigo (dye)	2	$0.25			
(Rose) Madder (dye)	1	$0.25	**Kitchen Related**		
Cashmere Vest Pattern	1	$2.00	Coffee Pot	1	$1.00
Pearl Buttons	1	$0.13 doz	Large Pitcher	1	$0.63
Hooks & Eyes	1	$1.86	Tin Bucket	2	$0.38
Pins	1	$0	Tin Pan	2	$0.34
Cotton	2	$1.13 bale	Candle Mold	2	$0.08
Thread	4	$0.04-0.13 spool	Small Tin	1	$0.06
			Glass Tumbler	1	$0.10
			Borax	1	$0.10
Clothing					
Coat, Pants & Vest	1	$13.39			

Table 5.2b - Product Sales List - Part 2

Category/Product	Sales	Price	Category/Product	Sales	Price
Medical Related			**Food & Tobacco**		
Fahnestock's Vermifuge	2	$0.25 vial	Coffee	12	$0.16 1/2 lb
Hair Restorer	1	$0.50 bottle	Tea	2	$2.00
Castor Oil	1	$0.25 bottle	Salt	2	?
Sanative Pills	1	$0.25 box	Sugar	1	$0.2 loaf
Jayne's Pills	1	$0.25 box	Bacon	1	?
Epsom Salts	1	$0.25 box	Eggs	1	$0.06 1/2doz
Bateman's Drops	1	$0.19 vial	Chocolate	1	$0.25
Thermometer	1	$1.50	Peppermint	1	$0.12
			Soda (baking?)	1	$0.25
Household Articles			Tobacco	3	$0.13 plug
Umbrella	2	$1.00-1.25			
Comb	3	$0.20-0.25			
Binding of Magazine	1	$1.25	**Horse Related**		
Novel	1	$0.25	Blind Bridle	1	$1.00
Paper	1	$0.04	Bridle Bit	1	$0.13
Cedar Pencil	1	$0.06	Whip Thong	1	$0.50
R(ubber) ball	1	$0.96			
Key Ring	1	$0.13	**Saddle-Making Supplies**		
Tooth Pick	1	$0.50	Hog Skins	1	$3.00
Broom Spat	1	$0.06	Red Skins	1	$0.42
Grass Bed Cord	1	$0.38	Straining Web	1	$1.37
			Pricking Teeth	1	$0.12 1/2 ea
Tools & Hardware			Patent bag	1	$0.50
Broad Hoe	2	$0.44	Large Buckles	1	$0.20 doz
Short Foot Shovel	1	$1.00			
Iron Plow Mold	1	$1.19			
Nails	1	$0.08	**Services Provided**		
Iron	3	$0.06 1/2 lb	Keeping Horse	1	$0.50 night
Cast Steel	1	$0.26 lb?	Rent of 1 Yoke Oxen	1	$1.15 day

Table 5.3 - Customer List with Professions

Name	Visits	Profession	Name	Visits	Profession
Anderson, Henry	1	Visitor	Larew, John M.	2	Farmer
Ashworth, John S.	2	Tanner	Larew, Mrs.	1	?
Baber, Hanton	2	Farmer	Lewis, Zebedee	1	Farmer
Baber, Powhatan	1	Farmer	Lively, Levi	1	Farmer
Barton, Willson	1	Farmer	McCartney, James H.	2	Inn Keeper
Beirne, Oliver	1	Farmer	Miller, John	1	?
Brown, Wm.	1	Laborer	Miller, Samuel	1	Farmer
Burke, Dr. Thos. J.	1	Physician	Monroe, James M.	4	Laborer
Callaway, Christopher	1	Laborer	Nisornon, Joseph (sp.?)	1	Visitor
Callaway, Garner	3	Shingle Maker	Pence, David	1	Farmer
Callaway, Joshua	1	?	Phillips, Samuel	7	Brick Layer
Camp, Wm.	1	Farmer	Prentice, James	6	Saddler
Campbell, Thos. S.	1	Owner RSS	Raffner, David S.	1	Visitor
Campbell, Wm. Jr.	1	Taylor	Roach, Isaac	1	Farmer
Campbell, Wm. Sr.	1	Farmer	Saunders, Holeman	1	Farmer
Cottle, Madison	1	Laborer	Seal, James W.	1	Wagon Maker
Cummins, John	1	Farmer	Shanklin, Absolom	2	Farmer
Dunlap, Addison	3	Farmer	Shanklin, Davidson	1	Farmer
Dunlap, Alex	1	Merchant	Shanklin, Rich. V.	1	Farmer
Dunn, Madison	1	Farmer	Spencer, Dr. Wm. W.	6	Physician
Eads, Joshua	3	Carpenter	Swinney, David	1	Farmer
Ellison, Isaac J.	2	Farmer	Swinney, Vincent	1	Farmer
Fowler, Dr. Thos.	1	Physician	Taylor, Henry	1	Farmer
Francis, John W.	2	Teacher	Taylor, Moses	1	?
Ganss, Arch	1	Visitor	Thrasher, Robert	2	Farmer
Gartin, Goodall	1	?	Vass, Boswell	1	Farmer
Goodall, Tiny	1	?	Vass, James	1	?
Gwinn, Sam'l	1	?	Vass, Maj. Wm.	2	?
Haynes, Alex D.	2	Merchant	Warrenburg, Wm.	3	Blacksmith
Haynes, Wm.	1	Merchant	Way Mrs.	1	?
Hutchinson, John M.	3	Carpenter	Wooden, E.W.	1	Baptist Preacher

William Burke's Continuing Role at The Red

In 1860, Burke published a pamphlet, "Red Sulphur Springs," in which he showed a continuing interest "since it passed out of my hands" in 1842. He explains, "I have since visited and practiced there, several years, and watched its effects on the human system in a variety of diseases, and although I have already given in detail my opinion of its properties and virtues in my work on the 'Virginia Springs,' yet, as the issue of that work was limited, and it may not be re-printed, I have thought it a duty I owed to humanity to place in the hands of the present Proprietors, for gratuitous circulation, the following treatise, embodying the joint experience of myself and my son, Thomas J. Burke, whose professional connection with those waters extends over a period of eighteen years" (p.3). Sections from this book on "Phthisis" (Tuberculosis) and "Curiosities and Scenery" are reproduced, in part, below.

"PHTHISIS, This disease as being the most formidable and destructive enemy of man first claims our attention. When it is acute and rapid in progress, running a course of a few months, it is wholly unmanageable, and the system falls prostrate before it. I beg the reader to bear in mind this distinction, and should he, under such circumstances, make the trial and fail, not to charge me with over-rating the power of the water, and encouraging a delusive hope. I say now at the outset, that the Red Sulphur is incapable of staying the destroyer in such a case. But if the attack is disposed to assume a chronic form, the deposition and development of tubercules being moderate and slow, and the constitution wrestling with the disease, then I say that this agent comes to the rescue, and in many cases triumphantly vindicates its power, either by affecting a cure, or by placing the system in such a condition as to protract life, and insure reasonable comfort for many years" (p.12). Burke goes on the give detailed testimonials of a number of doctors and former patients. In the following paragraphs, which are near the end of the pamphlet, he is appealing to the tourist in the visitors.

"CURIOSITIES AND SCENERY, The route by stage from Newbern (now Dublin) station, to the Red is uncommonly picturesque, for a great part of the way. The views from Cloyd Mountain, Salt Pond Mountain, and the great range of Peters Mountain in the distance, and Angel's Rest and the village of Pearisburg nestled near its base and the beautiful Kanawha, (here called New River) winding its quiet way, forming as it were, a succession of lakes embosomed in mountains, and forming varying objects of admiration, and then, most beautiful of all, the views at the crossing of the river in the batteaux, these, to the lover of nature, are well worth a day's travel. But these, varied and beautiful as they are, yield in grandeur to the view from the house of Mrs. Fowler, at the mouth of Indian Creek; five miles from the Red Sulphur. Indeed, the Kanawha, from its source to the Salines, is a never-ending kaleidoscope of nature." Note that batteaux were large wooden boats propelled by poles and designed to transport cargo.

Burke continues, "The curiosity that attracts most attention at the Spring is what may properly be called Nature's Gas Works. About half a mile above the Spring, on the verge of the Run, and under a slate-stone ledge, there issue several jets of gas, which when touched with a match, burn with a brilliant light. The proprietors have not turned it to account, but the day is not far distant when the valley of Red Sulphur, will be as fairyland, lighted up by this bountiful provision of nature."

"At Centreville, halfway between the Red and Salt Sulphur, there is a vast cave, called the Singing Cave. It is a mile and a quarter in extent—its northern opening visible from the road. It is well worth exploration" (p.23) So 1860, William Burke was still the promoter, as in the halcyon days of the thirties.

Chapter 6

The Civil War Years and the Fate of the Local Resorts 1861-1865

The Correspondence of the *Richmond Dispatch* for May 2, 1861, contains the following article on "Affairs in Monroe," sent from Sweet Springs and dated May 2, 1861.

"Old Monroe is all right--secession is in the ascendancy. Confederate and Palmetto flags are floating at every public place in the county. Monroe will go for secession overwhelmingly. The County Court has appropriated $10,000 for war purposes. A large southern flag, nine yards by fifteen, is to be erected at Red Sulphur Springs today. There are a few who condemn secession as a Democratic measure. If it is a characteristic peculiar to the Democratic Party to stand up for the rights of the South, for equality and independence, I thank God that I have always been an adherent to the principles of that party; but I rejoice in the fact, that there is too much patriotism in the south for secession to define a party measure." signed W.

Monroe and Greenbrier Counties were, retrospectively, "Border Counties" and it can be seen from the above quotation that they did not necessarily share the attitudes that prevailed in most of the nascent state of West Virginia. Indeed, Monroe sent all her thirteen companies to fight for the Confederacy; so while some individuals supported the Union, including soldiers, the general attitude of the populace was emphatically with the South (Kessel, 2001). The Greenbrier Valley contains much good farmland and slaves were used to a moderate extent. They constituted 12.5 percent of the population of Greenbrier County and 10.4 percent of Monroe in the 1860 census (Ziegler in White, 2013, p.1). These figures pale by comparison with the 30 percent figure in eastern Virginia, but still were evidently significant enough to drive the populace to secession.

Monroe County did not host any battles in the Civil War; but Greenbrier, which was more of a transportation hub and population center, saw a total of three stand-up fights. This region was of interest to the Federals because the counties to the west were friendly and because it was the shortest route to southern resources. The limestone country of the Border Counties was an important granary and source of livestock and also produced saltpeter, the main component in gunpowder. Perennial Union forays were designed to cross the Allegheny Mountains and attack the Virginia and Tennessee Railway, which President Lincoln called "The gut of the Confederacy." However the "homefield advantages" for the Confederates were that

Table 6.1 - Civil War Patients at Red Sulphur Springs

Name of Soldier	Military Unit	Date of Death	Comments
White, W.C.	Co A, 13th Ga	Nov 24, 1861	Floyd's Brigade
Argroves, M.M.	Co B, 13th Ga	Dec 5, 1861	"
Taylor, Sam'l	Co D, 13th Ga	Dec 8, 1861	"
Nicholson, James M.	Co I, 13th Ga	Dec 10, 1861	"
Smith, Green T.	Co I, 13th Ga	Dec 12, 1861	"
Young, Elisha	Co D, 13th Ga	Dec 16, 1861	"
Finch, H.G.	Co A, 20th Miss	Dec 12, 1861	?
Workman, David	Co L, 45th Va	Dec 4, 1861	Floyd's Brigade
Doss, Jesse	Co C, 45th Va	Dec 8, 1861	"
Sutphin, David	Co I, 45th Va	Dec 17, 1861	"
Baldwin, A.F.M.	Co G, 45th Va	Dec 19, 1861	"
Phipps, Sgt. George W.	Co C, 45th Va	Dec 20, 1861	"
Smith, Zachariah	Co L, 45th Va	Dec 24, 1861	"
Fox, Corp. Haywood	Co C, 45th Va	Dec 26, 1861	"
Gentry, John M.	Co C, 45th Va	Dec 26, 1861	"
Davis, Isaac N.	Co G, 36th Va	Sep 1, 1862	McCausland's Brigade
Maxwell, Solomon D.	Co G, 36th Va	Sep 2, 1862	"
Coon, Wm. R.	Co E, 36th Va	Sep 3, 1862	"
Ryan, Wm.	Co A, 36th Va	Oct 1, 1862	"
Tickle, Solomon D.	Co I, 36th Va	Oct 10, 1862	"
Umbarger, Andrew	Co G, 36th Va	Oct 28, 1862	"
Elkins, Wm.	Co A, 51st Va	Oct 16, 1862	Echol's Brigade
Terrel, Wm. B.	Co A, 50th Va	Nov 2, 1862	Echol's Brigade
Rippetoe, Lafayette	Co A, 22nd Va	Dec 4, 1862	William's Brigade
Shannon, Newson	Co G, 22nd Va	Dec 4, 1862	"
Meadows, Christopher	Co I, 26th Bn Va	Sep 25, 1862	Wharton's Brigade
Hughart, Dan'l	Co B, 26th Bn Va	Feb 25, 1863	"
Richie, Josiah	Co E, 26th Bn Va	Mar 21, 1863	"
Walls, Moses P.	Co C, 45th Va	Apr 21, 1863	William's Brigade
Burkett, Peter T.	Co K, 45th Va	Jun 3, 1863	"
Walls, William M.	Co C, 45th Va	Jun, 22, 1863	"

weather conditions in the mountains were often unpredictable and severe, supply lines were overextended, telegraph wires could be cut, and it was ideal terrain for bushwhackers. Troops advancing from the plains of Ohio had never experienced anything like it and were totally unprepared for the experience. Troops on both sides were often wet and without food and were often forced to steal from the local farmers, causing great hardships all around.

The resort springs of these counties were an obvious resource for the troops on both sides of the conflict because they could serve as campsites and hospitals, as well as rooms and headquarters for the officers. In this chapter, what is known of the fate of Red Sulphur Springs will be reviewed, and this will then be broadened to compare it with Salt Sulphur, Sweet Springs, and White Sulphur Springs during the Civil War. Grey Sulphur and Blue Sulphur Springs were already out of business by this time.

Red Sulphur Springs as a Military Hospital

The Civil War had begun by the time The Red opened as usual in June 1861, but the familiar advertisement also reassured readers that, "The RED SULPHUR is situated in a perfectly safe location in the mountains" (Richmond Dispatch, Jun 6, 1861, page 1). Later in the summer, Union forces moved across central western Virginia and put the Confederates into retreat, and General Henry Heth's Brigade was sent to Red Sulphur where he described the situation on Nov. 21: "I reached Pack's Ferry (on the New River) on the 20th. After a reconnaissance of that point and its immediate vicinity, I find no suitable place at which winter quarters can be erected. A want of sufficient ground and a great difficulty of obtaining firewood are the chief objections, not considering the insurmountable one of obtaining provisions and forage, in consequence of the impassable conditions of the roads 10 miles from Pack's Ferry toward the depot. I have concluded in compliance with your orders, to quarter this command at Red Sulphur Springs, which in my judgment complies with your orders as nearly as possible" (Kessel, 2001, p.10).

Heth went on to say, "The command is in no condition at present to erect buildings of any kind being without axes or tools of any description. These could doubtless be obtained sooner or later. In the meantime, however the sick list would be greatly increased. I suggest that the brigade be permitted to remain here until the necessary camp and garrison equipage can be obtained. Here we can find at least temporary shelter for the sick and the well, and the roads between this and the depot are at present passable." Note that the railway was still 38 miles away at Dublin, Va., and that winter weather conditions were unusually severe while "Typhoid was doing sad work among our soldiers at all the camps" (Morton, p.172).

Information available on Red Sulphur Springs during the war covers the winters of 1861-2 and 1862-3 and comes from a book titled *Cemeteries of Monroe* (Shumate et al., 1990, p.427-8). Actually, the data in Table 6.1 does not come from cemetery records but from old Confederate military records in the National Archives, and there is no guarantee that it is complete. Nonetheless it does contain basic information needed to relate the soldiers to the battles involved. The top panel contains soldiers who had been campaigning with General Floyd at the Battles of Carnifex Ferry and Cross Lanes and arrived with Henry Heth in November 1861. The total number of soldiers encamped at Red Sulphur that winter is unknown but probably was in excess of 1000. Of course, this was the off-season for the springs as well as the war, but the numbers would have far exceeded the room capacity of the hotel buildings.

The second winter saw the arrival of soldiers involved in the Kanawha Valley Campaign of General William W. Loring. Lowry's book on this subject relates this campaign directly to Red Sulphur as two of the four brigades used this as a base before and after the march to the Battle of Charleston (Lowry, 2016, pp. 77-9, 372-3, & 416-7). "Loring's forces were divided, with the brigades of Gen. John S. Williams and Col.

John McCausland at Red Sulphur Springs, Wharton's Brigade at Grey Sulphur Springs, and Echols' Brigade at the Narrows." He adds that the total force was "about 5,000 strong" so we can imagine that half of this number at The Red must have been a strain. There would have been a direct connection with the field during the September 6 to November 4 campaign to judge by when the patients arrived and some of them stayed well into the following summer before dying. No further advertisements for this resort were sent out, as the danger of travel must have exceeded the danger of staying in these mountains.

Military Activities at Other Resorts in Monroe and Greenbrier Counties

Ledgers survive through the Civil War at Salt Sulphur. For comparison, the number of visitors in 1860, just before the war, was 2,316 while only 277 persons registered during 1861 and this group consisted mainly of officers of the Confederate army with a few civilian guests from southern states (Table 6.2). In 1862 just 54, mostly military men, registered, while 299 came in 1863. Some of the military men were reported as sick, so the hotel may have served as a hospital although on a small scale. Salt Sulphur advertised for guests in 1861 and 1863, so this resort provides the most complete record we have in that respect.

The Old White was the largest resort of the group and the closest to the battles, so it did function as a major hospital in the first three years of the war. "Dr. O.A. Krenshaw was the medical director for the brigades of Wise and Floyd. On October 6, (1861), he informed Lee that he had more than 1,000 patients at White Sulphur Springs. Begging Lee to stop the flow of patients into his hospital, Dr. Krenshaw pointed out that overcrowding contributed to the spread of disease and increased the mortality rate. The hotel was overflowing with patients and all but the newest cottages had been taken over as hospital wards" (McKinney, 2004, p.126). The nearby battles, their dates, and proximity to White Sulphur are as follows: Lewisburg, May 23, 1862, 9 miles to the west; Dry Creek, August 26-27, 1863, just 2 miles to the east; and Droop Mountain, November 6, 1863, 37 miles northeast. As has been mentioned, Lewisburg was a major population center as well as transportation hub, so this is perhaps not surprising.

As for Yankee raids, only one occurred in November, 1863, and this affected Sweet Springs resort owner Oliver Beirne and many neighbors. This account is from Correspondence of the *Richmond Dispatch* (Feb 9, 1864). "I write to you this letter on the subject of Averill's raid in November, to notice some facts illustrating the cruelty and barbarity of the incursion of the enemy, not before brought to light. Mr. Beirne was treated with singular brutality. His houses were ransacked—his stores pillaged—all his meat (several thousand pounds) taken—all his liquors and wines appropriated by the plundering soldiery—his watch violently taken from his person—all his horses carried off. His place was well stripped of all that the Yankees desired or could convey away." Although both sides in the conflict were without food at times and engaged in open pilfering, this is one example of extreme conduct.

Most of the springs of Monroe and Greenbrier reopened by 1867 and the following account of White Sulphur provides some details on the extent of damages they had to contend with. "The Owners of White Sulphur Springs returned to their property soon after the war's end to survey damage to their investment and found the place a shambles. Fortunately, most of the buildings had withstood permanent structural harm, but the process of repairing steps, replacing furniture, fixing leaks, and cleaning up the grounds was extensive. The Confederate Government had paid rent and reimbursed the company for damages to the property while the buildings were used as a hospital; to meet earlier liens on the property the owners had sold off much of the furniture and supplies. This rent and sale income was placed entirely in Confederate bonds, and with the war's outcome those bonds proved worthless" (Conte, 1998, p.64-5).

"It took two full years to restore the property. The *Richmond Dispatch* was not optimistic about the prospects that summer of 1867. But the newspaper greatly underestimated both the determination and the fond memories of White Sulphur's clientele. Even for the defeated Southern states, life was not all politics and war. With amazing resilience old patrons returned again to their favorite spot, bringing in tow a whole new generation of young visitors filled with bright stories of glorious seasons before the war. It is surely an indication of how integral the resort was to the rhythms of Southern life that visitors came back in great numbers just a few years after bitter defeat" (Conte, ibid., p.65).

Table 6.2 - Calendar of Military Activity

Year	Season	Red Sulphur	Salt Sulphur	Sweet Springs	White Sulphur
1861	Summer	Open	Open	Open/Hospital	Open/Camp
	Autumn	Camp	Camp		Hospital
*****	Winter	Camp/Hospital			Hospital
	Spring		Camp		Battle/Hospital
1862	Summer		H.Q./Camp	Hospital	H.Q./Hospital
	Autumn	Camp/Hospital	Camp		H.Q./Hospital
*****	Winter	Camp/Hospital	Camp		H.Q./Hospital
	Spring	Hospital			Battle/Hospital
1863	Summer	Camp/Hospital	Open		
	Autumn		Camp	Raid/Camp	
*****	Winter		Camp	Camp	
	Spring				
1864	Summer			Raid	Occupation
	Autumn				
*****	Winter				
	Spring				
1865	Summer	Open by 1867	Open	Open/Hospital	Open in 1867

Red Sulphur Springs, West Virginia

Chapter 7

The Dunlap, Campbell, and Adair Owners and the Reconstruction Years, 1865-1879

After the Civil War, the citizens of the new state of West Virginia were required to sign a "Test Oath" that went like this, "I do solemnly Swear that I have never voluntarily borne arms against the United States, the reorganized government of Virginia, or the State of West Virginia; that I have never voluntarily given aid, comfort or assistance to persons engaged in armed hostility against the United States, the reorganized government of Virginia, or the State of West Virginia; that I have not at any time sought, accepted, exercised, or attempted to exercise, any office, or appointment whatever, under any authority, hostile or inimical to the United States, the reorganized government of Virginia, or the State of West Virginia; that I have not at any time yielded a voluntary support to any government, or pretended government, power or constitution within the United States, hostile or inimical to the reorganized government of Virginia, or the State of West Virginia; that I will support the constitution of the United States, and the constitution of the State of West Virginia; and that I take this oath freely, without any mental reservation or purpose of evasion" (Test Oath, *Shepherdstown Register*, W.V. Sep 30, 1865).

The above oath was patterned after the national "Voters Test Oath" imposed on the former Confederate states by the Republican dominated legislature over the objections of President Lincoln. Such a law effectively excluded most local citizens and virtually all former soldiers from serving in public office in the border counties, including Monroe and Greenbrier. In fact, it took until 1870 for more moderate legislation to evolve, so hard times were ahead and hard feelings were experienced during the period of Reconstruction (Rice, 1986, Chapter 13). Additionally, most people had their savings in Confederate currency which by the end of the Civil War had very little value.

Letter from West Virginia

By the 1870's, things had leveled off as we find in the following review of the situation at Red Sulphur Springs by a reporter visiting from the *Owensboro Examiner* of western Kentucky (Aug 16, 1878). "Your correspondent reached this point on Monday last, after a rather tedious trip (of 470 miles) occupying six

Table 7.1 Ownership Changes and Legal Records, 1865-1880

1865. Addison Dunlap seems to have been the sole owner of Red Sulphur during the Civil War period and into Reconstruction.

Aug 1867. Addison Dunlap must have been in financial trouble as the resort was resold to three individuals for $17,500 including himself, William Adair, prominent local merchant, and Robert D. Campbell, brother of former owners, Thomas and Isaac both deceased (Chancery Order Book 2, p.38).

Aug 1869. The owners must have defaulted on their payments as Red Sulphur was offered for sale by the Circuit Court (*Baltimore Sun*, Jul 8, 1870); however, no-one bought it.

Mar 1870. Addison Dunlap died, having been an owner since 1843.

Jun 1871. Red Sulphur was rented for the season by "Dunlap, Adair & Co." presumably Addison and William Adair (*Richmond Dispatch*, Jun 28). It seems that the Circuit Court must have required that it be rented by the erstwhile owners, in view of the fact that it had not been sold.

Jan 1874. The Springs were rented again, this time just by William Adair for $800 (*The Daily State Journal*, Alexandria, Nov 13, 1873).

Aug 1877. Red Sulphur Springs was again offered in a Commissioner's Sale (*Richmond Dispatch*, Aug 3, 1877), however, again, no one bought it.

Oct 1878. In a final Commissioner's Sale, Red Sulphur was again offered (*Richmond Dispatch*, Sep 26, 1878).

Oct 1880. Red Sulphur was finally bought on Oct 22, 1880, for just $9,500 by Levi P. Morton, financier, and eventual Vice President of the United States (Deed bk X, p.560). Technically, it was originally sold to Benjamin Wilson on Oct 16, 1879, on behalf of Morton and it reverted to Morton when he completed payment. Interestingly, the sellers were considered to be "Addison Dunlap, Thomas S. Campbell, Alexander D. Haynes, Richard V. Shanklin, Robert D. Campbell, Isaac H. Campbell, Alexander Dunlap, William Adair, their heirs, legatees, devisees and venders." Of these eight individuals, only three were alive.

days. It is proper, however, to say that two of the six days were not spent in traveling. The Springs are reached by traveling twelve miles over a rough mountain road, after leaving the railroad station. The Red Sulphur Springs are in Monroe County, W.Va., one hundred and sixty miles from Huntington, via the Chesapeake & Ohio railroad, and forty-four miles South of White Sulphur Springs, in Greenbrier County. The Springs are beautifully situated at the head of a small valley, surrounded by mountains, picturesque and grand. Nature, in fact, has done all that was necessary to render the spot attractive."

"The buildings, however, which are of many years standing, show evident marks of decay. The buildings were occupied as a hospital during the war, and that was certainly not calculated to improve their appearance or condition. They are, however, sufficiently well preserved to be pretty comfortable. The improvements were probably in their day, second to no watering-place in the country. The Springs property is in litigation at present, and should it fall into the hands of capitalists (in the form of carpet baggers) who would make the necessary expenditures to put everything in first-class order, there would be no trouble to secure the large annual attendance of visitors who came here in the past years."

"The Messrs. Adair, the present owners of the Springs, are polite and attentive, and ever ready to do anything in their power to contribute to the enjoyment of their guests, and I must say succeed very well with the facilities at hand. The water is not as strong as the Grayson Springs (eastern Kentucky). In fact, it is not strong enough to be at all objectionable to any one after using it a few times. The neighbors all around the springs come and drink the water. I have been told that when horses become accustomed to drinking the water, they will not drink any other. The visitors here, some fifty or sixty in number, are for the most part persons seeking relief from bronchial and lung diseases."

"There are persons here now who have been coming here regularly for long terms of years, and one gentleman who has been coming to this Mecca for consumption (tuberculosis) for the space of thirty years and is still a hale looking man although he has had over a hundred hemorrhages. The testimony of eminent medical men, and others who have put the merits of Red Sulphur water to practical test in past years, renders it quite certain that the water possesses in an eminent degree the qualities requisite to the healing of pulmonary diseases."

"As the company here is composed largely of invalids, and the place somewhat isolated, there is an entire absence of the display and show which are encountered at a fashionable watering place. It is just the place for a person to come who wishes to get the benefit of the water and have a good quiet time. The guests are very sociable, and indulge freely in croquet, horse-back riding, etc. making it more like a family on a large scale than anything else."

"There is a liberal sprinkling of preachers here during the season, there being sometimes as many as seven at a time, and as a probable consequence, a noon prayer meeting has been maintained for several weeks, a rather novel feature for a watering place. Rev. J.C. Molloy, of our city, has about completed his third week here, and speaks of remaining a week or so longer."

"Old Virginia probably contributes a majority of all visitors to this place, although several other states are represented. This is probably owing to the fact that the Springs are better known in Virginia than in other and more remote sections of the country. With this brief sketch, your correspondent will take leave of you for the present, signed, Yours truly, L.L." See also Figure 7.1 for the views of the new management.

Ownership in the Post-War Era

The legal complexities and courthouse references of this troubled time are outlined in Table 7-1. The one bright spot was in 1867 when the one surviving resort owner, Addison Dunlap, was joined by Robert D.

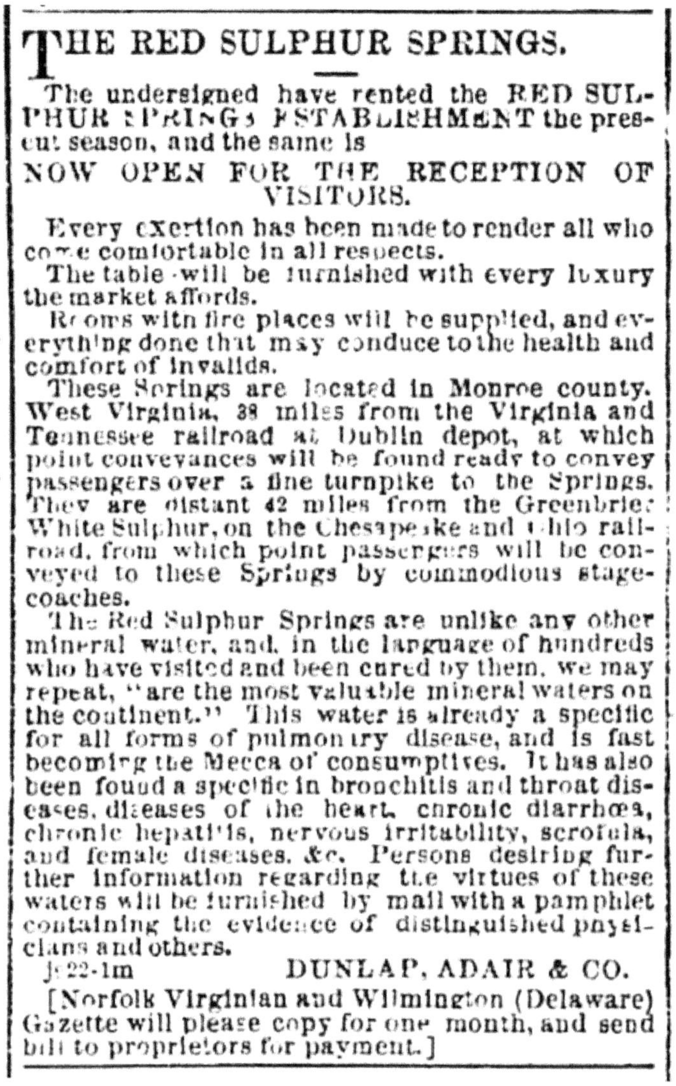

THE RED SULPHUR SPRINGS.

The undersigned have rented the RED SULPHUR SPRINGS ESTABLISHMENT the present season, and the same is

NOW OPEN FOR THE RECEPTION OF VISITORS.

Every exertion has been made to render all who come comfortable in all respects.

The table will be furnished with every luxury the market affords.

Rooms with fire places will be supplied, and everything done that may conduce to the health and comfort of invalids.

These Springs are located in Monroe county, West Virginia, 38 miles from the Virginia and Tennessee railroad at Dublin depot, at which point conveyances will be found ready to convey passengers over a fine turnpike to the Springs. They are distant 42 miles from the Greenbrier White Sulphur, on the Chesapeake and Ohio railroad, from which point passengers will be conveyed to these Springs by commodious stagecoaches.

The Red Sulphur Springs are unlike any other mineral water, and, in the language of hundreds who have visited and been cured by them, we may repeat, "are the most valuable mineral waters on the continent." This water is already a specific for all forms of pulmonary disease, and is fast becoming the Mecca of consumptives. It has also been found a specific in bronchitis and throat diseases, diseases of the heart, chronic diarrhœa, chronic hepatitis, nervous irritability, scrofula, and female diseases, &c. Persons desiring further information regarding the virtues of these waters will be furnished by mail with a pamphlet containing the evidence of distinguished physicians and others.

je 22-1m   DUNLAP, ADAIR & CO.

[Norfolk Virginian and Wilmington (Delaware) Gazette will please copy for one month, and send bill to proprietors for payment.]

Figure 7.1 This advertisement brings us into the post-Civil War Reconstruction Period, and here the emphasis is on the health-giving aspect of Red Sulphur Springs.
(*Richmond Dispatch*, Jun 28, 1871)

Campbell and William Adair, in re-purchasing The Red for $17,500. However, by 1869, Red Sulphur was again on the market in the form of a well-advertised auction sale by the Circuit Court. As a sign of the times, no one bought it until 1880 after it had been offered twice again in 1877 and 1878. In the meantime, newspapers advertised it was rented by "Dunlap & Adair" and then, just "Adair" after Dunlap died. Table 7-1 includes, at the bottom, a list of eight individuals considered to have a stake in the Red Sulphur Springs at the time of its eventual sale to Levi P. Morton in 1880. Four of these are discussed in Chapter Five and the other four are covered here.

Richard V. Shanklin (1805-1881), husband of Mary Pack, was the brother-in-law, and one of the executors of Alexander Dunlap. He joined the discussion in 1858 when the Campbell brothers, Thomas, and Isaac, were brought into the company. It eventually developed that the money they had promised to establish one-third ownership came from bonds executed by a third party and were flawed. It was not until May 1877 that the Supreme Court of Appeals of West Virginia decided, "In every aspect of the case we think that Shanklin, as executor of Alexander Dunlap, deceased, is entitled to the purchase money" (Dunlap's Ex'rs v. Shanklin, 10 WVa 662, 1877). However, this decision didn't have any effect on the management on Red Sulphur as both brothers had died before the Civil War.

Alexander Dunlap Haynes (1824-1857) was a nephew and also an executor of his namesake, Alexander Dunlap. He seems not to have played an official role at the Resort although he worked as a clerk in the A. Dunlap Store in the early 1850's.

Robert Dunbar Campbell (1818-1895) was a farmer, husband of Mary K. Johnson, and the younger brother of Thomas and Isaac; he became a co-owner in the 1867 sale of the Springs. He was also executor of Thomas' estate. His son wrote this piece about him. "In about 1877 or somewhere around that time, my father had signed a note for the Red Sulphur Springs Company, an accommodation note it was, and they recklessly spent everything they had and got behind and were sold out. All the people who signed these notes had to sell their farms, and father was one of them. This was a bad state of affairs at that day and time" (R.E.J. Campbell, 1948, *Random Recollections*, on file in the Monroe Co. Hist. Soc.). Actually, some of Robert's children and friends bailed him out, so he did not lose the farm. We should note that this situation came about during the Financial Panic that lasted from October 1873 to June 1879 (Aliber & Kindleberger, 2015, pp.195-6).

William Adair (1804-1887) was prominent in a large mercantile business near Red Sulphur when he became an owner in 1867 (Morton, 1916, p.298). He was married to Ann Harvey, daughter of James Harvey, early owner of the Resort. He had served as a Delegate from Monroe County in the Virginia Legislature in 1842-3 and as President of the Giles, Fayette & Kanawha Turnpike in 1859 (Martindale, 2017, p.52). At Red Sulphur, he served as a proprietor from about 1871 to 1878 (*Shepherdstown Register*, Feb. 18, 1887).

Visitors and Travel

The number of visitors coming to Red Sulphur Springs after the war declined sharply. We do have a rather disheveled ledger (Monroe Co. Hist. Soc. collection) from which we can extract numbers of parties for certain years; 115 parties for 1867, 208 for 1868, 236 for 1869, and 378 for 1870. This compares with 664 for 1834 and 897 for 1836 (see Chapter Three). So, the numbers had fallen from the heyday of the Springs, and the owners were struggling financially. Perhaps more interesting are the numbers as a function of the visitors' state of origin, and these are plotted on Table 3.2 in Chapter Three. The greatest concentration of parties was from West Virginia and Virginia (77%), while the remaining southern states (10%) were less well represented after the war than the North (16%). Of course, the economy of the south was in bad shape.

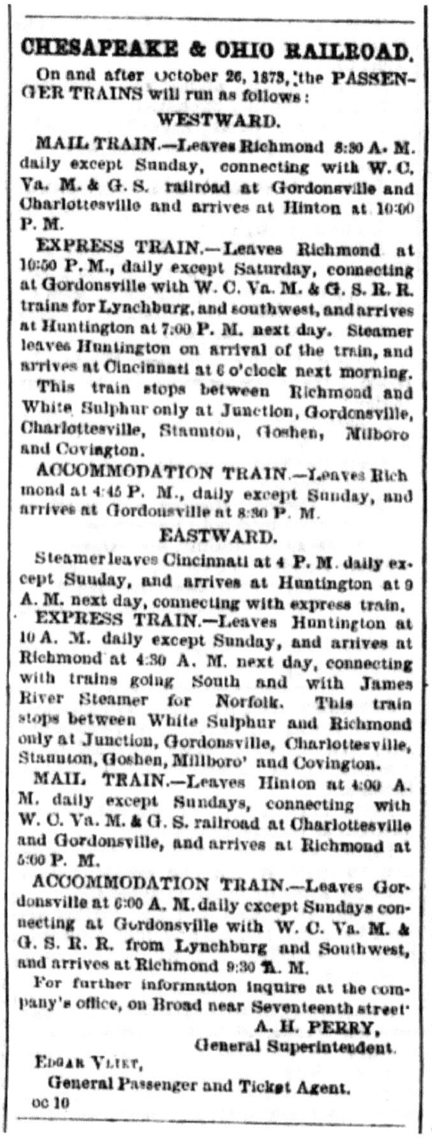

CHESAPEAKE & OHIO RAILROAD.

On and after October 26, 1873, the PASSENGER TRAINS will run as follows:

WESTWARD.

MAIL TRAIN.—Leaves Richmond 8:30 A. M. daily except Sunday, connecting with W. C. Va. M. & G. S. railroad at Gordonsville and Charlottesville and arrives at Hinton at 10:30 P. M.

EXPRESS TRAIN.—Leaves Richmond at 10:50 P. M., daily except Saturday, connecting at Gordonsville with W. C. Va. M. & G. S. R. R. trains for Lynchburg, and southwest, and arrives at Huntington at 7:00 P. M. next day. Steamer leaves Huntington on arrival of the train, and arrives at Cincinnati at 6 o'clock next morning.

This train stops between Richmond and White Sulphur only at Junction, Gordonsville, Charlottesville, Staunton, Goshen, Millboro and Covington.

ACCOMMODATION TRAIN.—Leaves Richmond at 4:45 P. M., daily except Sunday, and arrives at Gordonsville at 8:30 P. M.

EASTWARD.

Steamer leaves Cincinnati at 4 P. M. daily except Sunday, and arrives at Huntington at 9 A. M. next day, connecting with express train.

EXPRESS TRAIN.—Leaves Huntington at 10 A. M. daily except Sunday, and arrives at Richmond at 4:30 A. M. next day, connecting with trains going South and with James River Steamer for Norfolk. This train stops between White Sulphur and Richmond only at Junction, Gordonsville, Charlottesville, Staunton, Goshen, Millboro' and Covington.

MAIL TRAIN.—Leaves Hinton at 4:00 A. M. daily except Sundays, connecting with W. C. Va. M. & G. S. railroad at Charlottesville and Gordonsville, and arrives at Richmond at 5:00 P. M.

ACCOMMODATION TRAIN.—Leaves Gordonsville at 6:00 A. M. daily except Sundays connecting at Gordonsville with W. C. Va. M. & G. S. R. R. from Lynchburg and Southwest, and arrives at Richmond 9:30 A. M.

For further information inquire at the company's office, on Broad near Seventeenth street.

A. H. PERRY,
General Superintendent.

EDGAR VLIET,
General Passenger and Ticket Agent.
oc 10

Figure 7.2 This Chessie System advertisement is important because this line was new, making it the first time it was possible to get close to Red Sulphur by rail.
(*The Daily State Journal*, VA Jan 7, 1874)

The Chesapeake & Ohio Railroad was completed through the new state of West Virginia in 1873 and had reached the town of Talcott, within 12 miles of Red Sulphur, so this was quite a benefit to travelers. However, the remaining distance was by stagecoach, and one correspondent wrote, "The ride from Talcott Station over to the springs has not grown any shorter since I passed over it—The signpost just at the end informs you that the five hours or more on the road have been spent in making the 12 miles!" (*Alexandria Gazette*, Aug 14, 1877). For comparison, you could get all the way from Richmond to nearby Hinton in 13½ hours which is about 264 miles, so this would be clicking along at 21 mph, about four times faster than in pre-railroad days. The very first Chesapeake and Ohio schedule shows (Figure 7.2) that the Express Train could get you from Richmond to Huntington, WV, transfer you to the Ohio River steamboat and get you to Cincinnati in 31 hours. Admittedly, it would take longer to come the other way, because of the upstream current on the Ohio River. Fortunately, the stagecoach connection to the Springs was later improved by the addition of the Red Sulphur Turnpike from Lowell built by subsequent owner Levi P. Morton, but even then, the ride took three hours.

Interestingly, all of these difficulties might have been avoided, as pointed out by Oren Morton (1916, p.219). Indeed, "To a person familiar with the topography of Monroe, it seems rather strange that the Chesapeake and Ohio should have chosen the difficult route between Callaghan and Ronceverte, requiring long tunnels and heavy cuts and fills. From Covington to Petersburg there is one continuous valley. The water-gaps through which Second Creek escapes from its upper basin look as if specially designed for the railroad to use. It involves no very difficult work to follow Dunlap Creek to one of its sources, then pass through Second Creek gaps, and down Indian Creek to New River. Had this course been followed, the economic consequences would have been striking. Sweet Springs, Salt Sulphur, and Red Sulphur would have been on, or very close to the line of the railroad. The influence of White Sulphur and Lewisburg was the double magnet that drew the Chesapeake and Ohio into its difficult course."

Circuses and Tournament

We know of two visits by A. Robinson's South-Western Circus to Red Sulphur Springs during this period, one in August 1867 and one in August 1878 (Monroe Co. Hist. Soc. Ledger; *Alexandria Gazette*, 14 Aug.). A one circus write says "Following the White Tops was the phrase describing people who were in the circus. The first equestrian display dubbed a 'circus' in the United States was held in 1793 in Philadelphia, and one of the impressed patrons was President George Washington. By the 1860's, there were as many as two dozen or more large companies crisscrossing the United States and western territories. Most of them set off in spring, worked their way north and west through the summer, retreated south in the fall, and spent the winter resting up and preparing for the next season. The circus was also known as a 'wagon show' because the nomadic troupes traveled in wooden wagons, and some of them were transformed into stages featuring performers who did not require much space. With the so-called freak shows, for example, the 'acts' simply had to sit or stand on a platform and be ogled by amused or horrified patrons" (Clavin, 2019, pp.183-5).

A contemporary advertisement from Robinson's Circus is shown, in part, in Figure 7.3. Some of the acts were described as follows: "HIRAM DAY, clown and humorist, the embodiment of fun, wit, originality, and genuine humor, a living exemplification of the old adage, 'laugh and grow fat', MONS. CUTLER, in his great Cannon Ball act., HARRY JENNINGS, the great two, four and six horse rider, and PROF. HURLBUT with his trained horses which will be driven to a carriage, without bridle, reins, breeching or traces!" Such were the acts of the day, which had to travel into the mountains of West Virginia and entertain a combination of resort guests and farmers' families.

Figure 7.3 Robinson's Circus was one of the shows that toured the country and this one visited Red Sulphur more than once.
(*The Anderson, SC, Intelligencer*, Oct 16, 1867).

Local folks were capable of sponsoring spectacles as well, as seen by a jousting tournament at Red Sulphur on July 3, 1878, and described in the *Monroe Watchman* (July 5 issue) "The day was warm, a large crowd was present, the track was in excellent condition, and everything passed off pleasantly. The knights marched to the grounds in military order, being commanded by Major James F. Patton, Chief Marshall. The contest commenced about 11 A.M. Dr. McDonald, having first delivered the Charge of the Knights, in a few happy and appropriate remarks. After each knight had ridden four times, it was found that J.H. Crosier, L.P. Johnson, and C.E. Lynch had tied on the first honor, each one having taken 11 rings out of 12. After riding for ties was over, it was declared that J.H. Crosier, King of Jupiter, had won first honor. He afterwards crowned Miss Lelia Hodge, Queen of Love and Beauty. The successful knights are all Monroe boys. The Coronation took place at night in the High School Building. The Coronation Address was delivered by A.C. Houston, Esq. who performed this duty in his usual chaste and happy style, after which a beautiful crown and wreath were placed on the heads of the fair queen and her maids. The exercises were closed with a dance which was continued to the 'Wee sma' hours o'the nite', which all present very highly enjoyed." So, it sure seems that the local folks were able to put on quite a show.

Red Sulphur Springs, West Virginia

Chapter 8

Levi P. Morton, New York Friends, and an Era of Absentee Ownership 1880-1896

And now, for a change of pace. Morton was the son of a congregational minister in Vermont. He eventually settled in New York and became a successful merchant, cotton broker, and one of the country's top investment bankers, founding the Morton Trust Company. He also became involved in politics, rising to the level of Vice President of the U.S. He obviously had a lot of money, and this of course had been sorely needed at Red Sulphur Springs for years. He bought the resort in 1880, the year before he was appointed to be the United States Minister to France. At this time, Morton was a member of Congress and was friendly with fellow congressman Col. Ben Wilson of West Virginia. Wilson knew that Morton had a nephew with consumption, Frank Morton of Fairmont, WV, and he was the first to tell him about Red Sulphur (Clarksburg Daily Telegram, Jan 5, 1909). Morton seems to have balanced his local affairs with his political career, as he was involved in one way or another with The Red for 37 years (Table 8.1). In fact, by the time he first visited Red Sulphur five years after his purchase, he reportedly had invested $100,000.00 in improvements (Shepherdstown Register, Sep 4, 1885). This was during the years he was Minister to France.

The Honorable Levi P. Morton became Vice President in the Benjamin Harrison administration from 1889 to 1893 (Figure 8.1). According to *Encyclopedia Britannica*, "Harrison's administration was marked by an innovative foreign policy and expanding American influence abroad. Although the treasury had a surplus at the inception of Harrison's administration, the 'Billion-Dollar Congress' spent such enormous sums on soldier's pensions and business subsidies that the surplus soon vanished." The administration lasted just one term and terminated with the Financial Panic of 1893. This is ironic in that Morton had been very successful as a financier in private life. Morton's political career then moved to a term as Governor of New York State from 1895 to 1896. During these political sojourns, Morton seems to have taken out a lien on Red Sulphur and had New York associates take over control of the resort (Table 8.1). Indeed, during this interval, it changed hands several times and was placed in trust twice, so evidently times were rough during the financial downturn. None of these owners seem to have taken much interest in Red Sulphur, although there is a record of William Noble and wife visiting in 1889 (See Appendix Seven). Also, the Nobles' founded

Table 8.1 Property Transactions and Political Offices - Levi P. Morton Era, Part 1

The legal transactions presented here are summarized in Monroe County Deed Book 33, pp.60-63, and the entire document is transcribed in Appendix Six for reference. RSS is used as an abbreviation below, and the 1200-1300 acreage is consistent throughout.

1880. Frank Hereford, Commissioner sold RSS to Levi P. Morton of New York for $9,500 (Deed Bk. X, p.560).

1881. Aug to May 1885, May, L.P. Morton was the United States Minister to France.

1885. Sept., L.P. Morton paid his first visit to RSS (*Shepherdstown Register*, WV, Sep 4).

1888. June, Levi P. & Anna L. Morton conveyed RSS to Chas. H. Lindsley of New York City for $10 and reserved a lien to secure to him the payment of $25,000 lent to the Lindsleys (Deed Bk. 28, p.154). On the same day, Chas. H, & Silvia A. Lindsley executed a trust deed on 1300 acres to Wm. Morton Grinnell, Trustee, to secure the $25,000 to Levi P. Morton (Bk 1, Monroe Courthouse, p.287). Grinnell was a New Yorker and nephew of Morton.

1888. Nov.6, Levi P. Morton was elected Vice President of the United States.

1889. Chas. H. & Silvia A. Lindsley sold RSS to Elizabeth Coates of Albany, NY for $21,000 (Deed Bk. 28, p.358), Elizabeth Coates, in turn, sold RSS to William Noble of NY City for "$1.00 and other valuable consideration" (Deed Bk. 29, p.62).

1890. Wm. & Eliz. Noble conveyed the property to the Red Sulphur Springs Water Co., a new company founded by Noble and based in NY City for "$1.00 and other valuable consideration" (Deed Bk. 29, p.66; Red Sulphur Springs Water Company, 1898). The RSS Water Company, in turn, conveyed the RSS in trust to the Holland Trust Co. of New York State (Trust Deed Bk. 2, p.5).

1890. Wm. Noble, President of the RSS Water Co. granted Power of Attorney for the Water Co. to Frank Hereford, Commissioner of Monroe County WV (Deed Bk. 29, p.20).

1893. Mar.4, The Vice Presidential term of L.P. Morton ended.

1895. Jan.1, L.P. Morton was elected Governor of New York State.

1896. Nov.24, The RSS Water Co., with Wm. & Eliz. Noble, conveyed the RSS to Levi P. Morton and wife; and Morton released the lien for $25,000. The Holland Trust company had been unable to sell any bonds and returned them to the RSS Water Company (Deed Bk. 33, p.60).

1896. Dec.31, L. P. Morton's term as Governor ended.

Chapter 8   71

the Red Sulphur Water Company during this interval and turned it over to Morton when he regained ownership.

As has been said, Morton visited Red Sulphur Springs in 1885 and "while suggesting improvements and making plans, he remarked that he intended trying the experiment of a tobacco patch. Before leaving he directed that, one hundred acres of his best land be cleared up and prepared for the raising of tobacco" (*Wheeling Daily Intelligencer*, 1885, Nov 30). By 1972 it was reported that many tobacco barns had been erected and Monroe County produced about 81,384 pounds of burley tobacco (Motley, p.,140). This and other examples show that Levi P. Morton was a philanthropist with a soft spot for the farmer, gained perhaps from his origins in rural Vermont.

Figure 8.1 President Benjamin Harrison and Vice President Levi P. Morton, 1888-1893.
(Library of Congress)

Table 8.2 Red Sulphur Springs General Information, 1890-2

Correspondence File of Dr. J.K.P. Gleeson, Manager

Season Length

    July 1st – end of August?

Transportation

    Train: Washington, DC to Lowell, WV – 8 hrs. 55 min. (overnight) at $18.00 return

    Stagecoach: Lowell Station to Red Sulphur Springs – 2 ½ to 3 hrs. (12 miles)

Room/Charges

    Weekly Rates $12.00 to $25.00 (depending on location and number of beds)

    Monthly Rates $45.00 to $85.00 (as above)

Advertising

    In the following cities:-New York, Philadelphia, Baltimore, Washington, Richmond, Cincinnati, Louisville, Owensboro, and Indianapolis (from a list of newspapers)

Services

    Three Musicians to play on the lawn, porches, and ballroom, depending on weather

    Carriages for visitors' use include a Phaeton, Surrey, & Wagonette (based on an order)

    Barber Shop Services provided

    Telegraph connections available to Lowell Railroad Station

    Hot or Cold Sulphur Bath for use at 35 cents

    Red Sulphur Water can be shipped at $4.00 per case of 20 bottles

Philosophy

    "This is a health, not a pleasure resort"

The Gleeson Correspondence Ledger (1890-1892)

This ledger has been conserved in the files of the Monroe County Historical Society. It is a remarkable binder of 300 pages of a tough tissue paper. This paper was porous enough so that a sheet of letter paper could be slipped beneath the tissue sheet and the ink writing would penetrate through to the letter paper and leave a copy on the lower level; this worked like carbon paper except the letter was on bottom while the copy was on the top. The system worked reasonably well, although some of the tissue sheets are blotchy and hard to read. The ledger belonged to Dr. J.K.P. Gleeson, Medical Director and Manager of the Red Sulphur Springs Water Company, as well as stockholder of four shares at $25.00 each (Red Sulphur Springs Water Company, 1891). The letters range from orders for food items and other products, enquiries from visitors planning reservations, and from cooks or musicians wanting jobs, and other diverse matters of interest. For instance, there is a letter dated Aug 4, 1891, to Miss R. Pearce, Flushing, NY, saying, "I have to tell you that Mr. Morton, nephew of Hon. L.P. Morton is dead." Little clues like this help understand why Morton, Vice President by this time, was interested in the medicinal aspects of the resort.

The contents of Table 8.2 were gleaned from the correspondence ledger. We see for instance, by this date one could get from Washington D.C. to the Lowell Station in just under 9 hours, 4 ½ hours less than it took to travel the lesser distance from Richmond two decades earlier. Table 8.3 lists the states from which enquiries were received so this list may be compared with the number of parties in the register of earlier chapters although the source is not precise. We still find that the source of visitors is quite broad and similar to before the war although by this time, the railroads were approaching modern standards of comfort and speed. Finally, Table 8.4 lists food items ordered from establishments around the eastern part of the country. The fresh fish from Norfolk, VA is perhaps surprising but possible with improvements in the rail system. Note also, Acker, Merral & Condit of New York, a company that is still in business.

Table 8.3 - Visitor Travel Data for 1891

State of Origin North to South	1891 % of Parties	Airline Distance to Red Sulphur
New York	5	440-500 Miles
Pennsylvania	2	340
Indiana	1	370
Ohio	15	129-230
Virginia	40	35-250
West Virginia	7	35-160
North Carolina	4	160
Georgia	5	300-425
Alabama	5	490-625
Kentucky	15	350-425
Tennessee	1	340

Table 8.4 - Food Items Ordered for Red Sulphur Springs, 1891
From the Correspondence file of Dr. J.K.P. Gleeson, Manager

Pickett & Company, Norfolk, VA

20 lbs. Bluefish

200 Clams

2 doz. Fine (Norfolk) Spots

10 lbs. Spanish Mackerel

20 Gray Trout

Ruffner Brothers, Charleston, WV

2 crates of Ham

1 barrel of Salt Pork

1 case of French Peas

20 lbs. Chocolate

50 lbs. Salt Codfish

2 doz. Corn Starch

Acker, Merral & Condit, New York

4 doz. cans of Lobster

4 doz. cans of Shrimps

4 doz. cans of Salmon

4 doz. cans of Plums

4 doz. cans of Peaches

24 Smoked Beef Tongues

2 doz. gallon cans of Tomatoes

C.W. Antrim & Sons, Richmond, VA

1 keg Olives

1 box Lemons

Significantly, Table 8.2 ends with the statement made by Dr. Gleeson that "This is a health, not a pleasure resort." It must be noted here that, just earlier in 1882, Robert Koch, the German researcher, discovered *Mycobacterium tuberculosis* which both established the germ theory of the disease and demonstrated that tuberculosis is contagious (Snowden, 2019, Chapters 14-15). Throughout the history of Red Sulphur, this disease was stressed as the place to go for this affliction, so dominant in the nineteenth century. So, it's interesting to examine the advertising of Red Sulphur to see what the reaction might have been to this discovery. Surprisingly, tuberculosis was still the focus of the advertising by this date. Snowden (pp.281-4) continues, "Indeed, one of the ironies of a disease that was painful, deforming, and lethal was that it was popularly deemed not only to affect men and women of high social standing, ability, and refinement, but also to augment and elevate their beauty, genius and sex appeal. For women, pulmonary consumption promoted a new anemic ideal of female beauty in its own image—thin, pale, delicate, elongated, and almost diaphanous." An example he uses is the character Mimi, in Puccini's opera, La Boheme. The "impact of tuberculosis in men was to bring their creative power to new heights. In this regard we see, Keats served as the ideal type of the male artist whose full creativity was said to have reached its fruition in the crucible of his fevered final year in Rome. There, fever consumed his body, allowing his mind and soul to soar to new heights that, free of disease, they would never have attained." In earlier years, the health issues were stressed at Red Sulphur even though young single men were part of the clientele. Perhaps the stress on health in Gleeson's comment was meant to discourage the "gay young blades" in view of the contagion that then became evident. Gleeson did say in his ledger, "I hope to make a regular sanitarium out of this place."

The Red Sulphur Turnpike

Levi P. Morton built this turnpike to ease travel from the C&O Station at Lowell to The Red. It was mentioned in Chapter Seven that complaints were received when the station at Talcott was used as it took five hours to travel the remaining distance by stagecoach. The turnpike was completed by 1882, to judge by advertisements, so then travel was only three hours, as the ferry crossing of the Greenbrier River became unnecessary and the turnpike followed a direct course, subparallel to the border of Summers and Monroe Counties. A detailed newspaper account of the multiple uses of this road was produced by Lester Lively (*Hinton Daily News*, date unknown) who quoted local resident Charles A. "Bud" Dunn (1885-1959). Dunn lived in the farm originally established by Nicholas Harvey, founder of Red Sulphur resort, and described by Crabtree and Ziegler (2021, p.159) and is at the crossing of Route 12 and Indian Creek. This farm had been used as the stable for the resort for many years and is where the stagecoach routes emanated.

In addition to passengers who were conveyed along the Red Sulphur Springs Turnpike, Dunn said, "Supplies for the farms were brought in over the road to the many stores which were built along the way. One of these, S.F. Humphreys, who operated at Red Sulphur, often brought in carload lots and supplied other merchants. It is said that Humphreys was the banker for the region. Those who had money and were afraid to keep it about them would place it in his hands for safe keeping. Banks were not close about in those days and did not have the confidence of many of the people. It is said that Humphreys once ordered a carload of mules shipped to Lowell. These were unloaded and driven over the Turnpike to the Red where they were placed in a corral. The next morning every blasted mule had jumped out and was found in a man's cornfield about half a mile away."

"Lumber, staves, tanbark and cross ties were hauled over the Turnpike for loading at Lowell. In the early part of this century, it was a common sight to see wagon after wagon pulled by horses, mules and oxen go by on a morning and return empty with a great clatter and the shrieking of rubber blocks as the brakes were applied on the downgrade."

"Tobacco was raised extensively in the area in years past which was packed in hogsheads and transported to the C & O for shipment to the markets. Lowell was also the loading point for cattle and sheep which were driven in great numbers over the Turnpike where they were weighed at the Gwinn scales and loaded out for the eastern markets."

"The most unusual caravan that used the pike was that of turkeys. Thousands of turkeys would be gathered together and driven on foot to Lowell where they were loaded into cars and shipped alive to the markets for butchering. It is said that some of these caravans consisted of as many as four thousand turkeys. They would be driven with one man in front with corn, who would drop some occasionally to toll them along, and others coming along behind to round up the stragglers. At nightfall the turkeys would take to the trees and the drivers would make their camp and be on hand the next morning bright and early to continue the drive when the turkeys came down off their roost."

"The building of the bridge across the Greenbrier at Talcott and as it became a free-bridge in about 1912 and most of the traffic was diverted to Talcott. The portion of the Turnpike from the top of Gwinns Mountain to the intersection with the Creamery Road was discontinued. That portion today is only a mark in the woods as large trees are found growing over the original roadway. However, the rest of the Red Sulphur Turnpike, tho shorn of its luster continues to serve the people of this area." It should be noted that in 2024 this humble road is still marked by a sign, "Red Sulphur Turnpike," while most of the earlier turnpikes are not so recognized. In summary, travel from rail to The Red began in 1873 and was from Talcott Station by ferry to Lowell, then from Lowell by the turnpike in 1882, and finally from Talcott by bridge to the abbreviated turnpike in 1912.

Overflow Problems at The Springs

More recently, Helen Ellison wrote of The Red (1991), "Not all arrived in carriages, elegantly dressed, and with servants. Some people came wearing jeans or homespun on horseback; some in spring wagons; or on Shank's Mare (walking). Neighboring farms kept the overflow and the less affluent. Some camped in their wagons or lived in rough wood shelters nearby. The reputed healing power of the water drew rich and poor alike." Because of the overcrowding problems at the big resorts many smaller establishments sprang up. An advertising brochure entitled "Ideal Summer Homes!" and published by the *Monroe Watchman* provided a comprehensive idea of all the accommodations in Monroe County in 1894, including resorts, hotels, and smaller establishments. Sweet Springs, Salt Sulphur, and Red Sulphur could accommodate 600, 250, and 250 respectively at that time. Intermediate-sized Union Hotel; Lynnside Boarding House at Sweet Springs; and Alderson Hotel, could house 40, 60, and 75 respectively. There were 17 mostly private homes that were open in the summer, and of these, six boasted nearby mineral springs. These could accommodate a total of 370 people, so altogether this added up to a grand total of 1645 guests that could be accommodated simultaneously. Indeed, Monroe was quite the tourist venue during the nineteenth century. You could enjoy "In the Heart of the Alleghanies... Magnificent Mountain Scenery... Life-giving Mineral Waters... and The Purest Air in the World... A Real Refuge of Rest and Recreation. Where mountain breezes blow, and roses bloom, and health and happiness hold high carnival" (again, quoting *The Monroe Watchman*).

Chapter 9

Levi P. Morton and the
Final Years of Red Sulphur Springs
1896-1927

Early in the twentieth century, a detailed brochure was released promoting the resort and describing many new improvements. (J.L. Dillion, Proprietor, Red Sulphur Springs, about 1909) The relevant pages, 13-14, are transcribed below and they speak of a number of developments.

"Red Sulphur Springs is situated in the southwestern portion of Monroe County, West Virginia, near the left bank of Indian Creek, some five miles from its confluence with the New River. It is reached by a ride of forty-five minutes in the hotel automobile from Talcott, on the Chesapeake & Ohio Railway, or from Lurich on the New River division of the Norfolk & Western Railroad, and Rich Creek Station on the Virginia Railroad. Sleeping and parlor cars are on the trains which leave Cincinnati or New York in the afternoon, and Washington or Richmond in the evening, arriving at Talcott the next morning. The mountain road, through picturesque scenery and forests or the odorous pine and maple, has been placed in excellent condition, and the new automobile service made expressly for the comfort of our patrons."

"The Red Sulphur estate is a magnificent tract of fourteen hundred acres, embracing in its boundaries every variety of mountain scenery (Figure 9.1). The hotel is situated in a narrow valley two thousand feet above sea level. It possesses accommodation for nearly four hundred guests and is nicely furnished and fitted up with modern conveniences. Wide verandas, three-fourths of a mile in measurement, run the whole length of the building on each floor, looking out on a smooth lawn studded with gigantic trees. From the veranda of the dining-room it is but a few feet to the spring's house—one of the handsomest of its kind in the country."

"The hotel is connected with Talcott by telephone. The charge for board ranges from $10.50 to $17.50 per week, according to location. Transient guests, $2 to $3 per day. Special terms for families and permanent guests."

"For the convenience of guests using the Sulphur baths, bathrooms with new porcelain tubs have been installed in the North wing of the hotel, and equipped with every modern improvement and of easy access from all bedrooms without leaving the hotel. A new dining-room building, 42 x 183 feet, with ballroom and bedroom on second floor and also a handsome building, known as the President's cottage, has just been

78   Red Sulphur Springs, West Virginia

Figure 9.1 Line Drawing of Red Sulphur Springs in the 1890's.

completed. A covered walkway, connecting main building of hotel with dining-room building, has been built. The hotel and grounds have been thoroughly renovated and modernized in every respect, and many improvements, including improved bowling alleys and barber shop. A new telephone line has been built, connecting with Western Union, at Talcott on C. & O. Railway; Lurich, on N. & W. Railway, and Rich Creek Station on the Virginia Railway."

"The hotel is conducted under the personal supervision and management of the Proprietor, Mr. J.L. Dillion, whose connection with prominent New York Hotels (among these, the New Grand, at Broadway and Thirty-first Street) has earned for him a wide reputation as a successful caterer, which is a guarantee that the patrons of Red Sulphur Springs will receive every courtesy and attention necessary to their comfort and welfare."

"Every possible attention will be paid to guests, and such methods adopted in each case, as to the use of the water, diet, rest and exercise, as will lead to the best possible results during their stay at the springs. For the recreation of the pleasure-seeker there is an excellent livery, bowling alleys, lawn-tennis court, croquet, automobiling, etc. Good shooting on the estate and good fishing within an easy distance. A good band enlivens the lawn in the afternoon, and a string band plays in the ballroom in the evening."

In summary, a fair amount of money must have been invested in The Red following its reacquisition by Levi P. Morton in 1896. The construction program included covered walkways between the buildings, and these were on two levels, to judge by photographs (Figures 9.2 to 9.5). The famous Society Hall on the terrace above the cottage rows is not present in an 1882 diagram of the grounds and was replaced by a dining room over twice as long near the spring house. And the room cost had been lowered since the 1890-92 ledger of Dr. Gleeson (Table 8.2).

The rail service connections had been improved and expanded. A bridge had been installed across the Greenbrier River at the C & O terminal at Talcott and an automobile service established, lowering the travel time to the resort from 2 ½ hours to forty-five minutes. Rail lines had opened on both sides of the New River, the Norfolk & Western on the west side in 1883, and the Virginia Railroad on the east side in 1908 (Reger & Price, 1926, pp.12,18). These made access from southern locations more efficient, although the N & W required the use of the Toney Ferry to cross the New River until 1925 (W.E. Trout, 2003, p.66). Finally, the exciting new activity of "automobiling" had been introduced.

Morton Offers Red Sulphur to the State

In January of 1909, Levi P. Morton sent a telegram to Governor Dawson of West Virginia offering to donate the Red Sulphur Springs and ten acres for use as a sanitarium. This comes as a surprise in view of the relatively recent improvements previously outlined. This move may have been in response to the failure of the Monroe Railroad Company chartered in 1904 to establish a link from Peterstown on the Virginia Railroad, and through Red Sulphur Springs to Ronceverte on the Chesapeake & Ohio Railroad (Hinton Daily News, 1904, Jan 9, page 1). It is difficult to imagine such a railway succeeding through such unsuitable terrain because the valley is less than 200 feet wide with 500-foot walls; so it would be completely filled with noise and smoke every few hours—not very suitable for a resort or a sanitarium.

Morton's offer generated a lot of excitement in the press because there was an alternate sanitarium site, Terra Alta in Preston County that was lacking in any facilities, so the cost to the state would have amounted to $150,000. However, Terra Alta was in Governor Dawson's home county, so politics was an issue. There were a number of positives for Red Sulphur Springs, including the fact that the water was thought to ease the symptoms of tuberculosis, if not cure it, and there was a record of over a hundred years to prove it. And

80 Red Sulphur Springs, West Virginia

Figure 9.2 Original Hotel and Pavilion, West Side of Fitz Creek Valley.

Figure 9.3 Carolina House, Batchelor's Row, and Philadelphia Row,
Left to Right on East Side of Valley.

Albert Sydney Johnston, editor of the *Monroe Watchman* was the person who had suggested the gift of Red Sulphur Springs to Levi Morton. Negatives for The Red included the fact that only ten acres were to come with the offer and more would have had to be bought from Morton; and further this was too steep to do much with (*Clarksburg Daily Telegram*, 1909, Jan 23, p.1; Raleigh Herald, Jan 28, p.1).

The Clarksburg paper also mentioned that "...for some time the Red Sulphur Springs had been run both as a health and pleasure resort, but the combination proved disastrous from a business standpoint, those who visited the place for pleasure and an outing were afraid of contagion and this class of visitors continued to dwindle." So, it does seem that nearly three decades after Robert Koch's research discovery, the truth of the infectious nature of tuberculosis was becoming broadly known. It was also known that tuberculosis was the leading cause of death in the country at the rate of 75,000 per year (Snowden, 2019, p.270). So the offer of Red Sulphur Springs to the state of West Virginia was not accepted.

Ownership at the End

Levi P. Morton finally gave up ownership of Red Sulphur Springs in 1917 by selling the resort to J.E. Hansbarger and several local colleagues (see Table 9.1 for names and references). The announcement came with a fair amount of excitement, "THE RED SULPHUR SPRINGS HOTEL will open on July 1, 1917, one of the famous hotel resorts of the world. This property has been purchased by local people, who have made extensive improvements, thoroughly renovated and disinfected the entire buildings" (*Louisville Courier Journal*, Jun 17, 1917, p.20). And there were celebrations, "Red Sulphur Springs was formally opened for the season Saturday and Saturday night and a delightful dance was given by the management. Between three and four hundred visitors attended the festivities, and the event was a great success. An orchestra from Bluefield furnished the music." The article goes on to name the guests from Hinton as this article was published by the *Hinton Daily News* (Jul 9, 1917, p.1).

The country was at war in Europe by this time, and things evidently did not go as smoothly as expected. Indeed, twenty lots were sold off in the first year, but there were plenty to spare as there were well over a thousand acres to begin with, and most of the land was too steep for anything but lumbering. Also J.E. Hansbarger was president of the First National Bank of Peterstown (Crabtree & Ziegler, 2021, p.103) so he probably was anxious to move the money. By November, 1918 it was announced in the Hinton Daily News (Nov 9, P.1) "RED SULPHUR MAY FALL TO THE GOVERNMENT. The owners made a tender of the property through Hon. Hubert Blue, Surgeon General of the United States Public Health Service, on a sale basis for an Invalids or Tubercular Government Hospital for returning soldiers." The property could be leased for $5,000 or sold for $50,000, and the offer was not accepted. The property continued to be sold in lots locally, and the hotel and 122 acres were sold to S.W. Harrell of Roanoke, VA and P.H. Rorer of Bluefield, WV. In 1921, but whether they ever ran it as a hotel is unknown. A tourist, Mrs. J. H. Pollock, visited The Red in 1925, took a few pictures, and wrote, "though the spa had been closed for years, some of the buildings were yet standing, and in fairly good condition at that time" (M.C.H.S. collections). The resort was eventually sold in 1927 to a local, Judge Charles W. Campbell, who proceeded to dismantle the buildings and sell the lumber (Figure 9.6).

The End of the Springs Era

There were at least 114 mineral springs concentrated in the boundary area shared by Virginia and West Virginia in the nineteenth century. This was demonstrated by Stan Cohen who spent many months searching for the remains of resorts from the Blue Ridge to the Allegheny Front and beyond and published

Figure 9.4 Campus Walkways and Period Dress ca. 1890's.

Figure 9.5 Elevated Walkways Added by Levi P. Morton.

a compilation with splendid vintage pictures of three- to five-story hotels with mile-long verandas adorned with ladies in elegant gowns and gents in bowler hats (1981). The text is good too, and quoted here are a couple of paragraphs describing the end of an era. "One can go back thousands of years and find evidence of people 'taking the waters.' The early Roman baths, especially at the Caracalla site in Rome, are world famous. Wherever the Romans went in their conquests, they sought out the mineral waters. All over Europe, springs were used and developed from the first days of human civilization. Names like Wiesbaden and Baden Baden in Germany; Aix la Chapelle in France; Bath, Brighton and Harrowgate in England and Spa in Belgium—which gave the world the name for these grand and glorious establishments—these names conjure up dreams of days gone by."

Cohen has some useful thoughts on when and why the end came. "A number of factors contributed to the demise of the spas through the years. Three main reasons for the closure of most of them are: the destruction that happened during the Civil War and the changing social systems in the South after the war; better treatment and newly discovered cures for diseases, especially after 1900; and, last, the start of the automobile age in the early 1900s which changed the fabric of American life. Cars gave people the mobility to travel from mountains to beaches or wherever they wanted to go, and summering at the spas was no longer fashionable." And so we went from mom & pop tourist courts, to campgrounds, to tourist homes, and ended up with Interstates and Holiday Inns, and one might ask, is this truly progress?

Figure 9.6 All That is Left - The Depression Under the Spring House.

Table 9.1 - The Demise of Red Sulphur Springs, 1896-1932 - Levi P. Morgan Era, Part 2
(RSS is used as an abbreviation)

1896. Morton finished his single term as Governor of New York State, and William and Elizabeth Noble returned the RSS to his ownership (see Appendix 6).

1909. Morton offered to donate the RSS with ten acres to the State of West Virginia for use as a sanitarium, but it was turned down.

1917. Morton sold the RSS to J.E. Hansbarger and associates for $20,000, including three notes of $5,000 each (Deed Bk. 50, 529). These new owners proceeded to sell the outlying lots, including as many as 20 lots in the first year.

1918. Hansbarger et al. offered to sell the RSS to the U.S. government for use as a hospital. It could be leased for $5,000 per year or purchased for $50,000 (*Hinton Daily News*, Nov. 9, 1918).

1920. Hansbarger et al. sold the "hotel and 122 acres" to S.W. Harrell of Roanoke and P.H. Rorer of Bluefield, W.V. for $15,000 (Deed Bk. 53, p.579).

1921. Harrell and Rorer executed a trust deed to P.H. Dillard and H.M. Moomaw, Trustees (Trust Deed Bk. 10, p.635). There evidently was default because Mountain Trust Bank of Roanoke eventually sold the property in 1927 (see below).

1923. RSS was proposed as a federal women's prison (*Hinton Daily News*, Sep 5, 1923).

1927. Local West Virginian Judge Charles W. Campbell bought the RSS from Mountain Trust Bank (Deed Bk. 61, p.12). Judge Campbell proceeded to dismantle the RSS buildings and sell the lumber (Dumont, p.29).

1930. Lewis M. Campbell bought the remaining property from brother, Charles (Deed Bk. 63, p.384).

1932. A building on the site of the RSS hotel was burned (*Hinton Daily News*, Aug 15, 1932). Also, about this time, the big store at Red Sulphur burned (Dumont, p.29). It is possible that these two buildings were one and the same.

Chapter 10

Earth Science and the Origin of the Minerals in the Springs

Turning again to Cohen's book on the *Historic Springs of The Virginias*, "the springs region actually encompassed the entire length of the Appalachian chain from New York to Alabama, but most of the resorts were concentrated in the Blue Ridge Mountains of Virginia and along the Allegheny Front of West Virginia." So, in this final chapter we will examine the central area of this great mountain chain from the earth science point of view (your author is a professional geologist and can't resist this opportunity). This will include the initial building of the mountains and their relatively recent reactivation, the reason for the cool mountain air, the chemistry of the springs, and the origin of their contained minerals.

Building The Appalachian Chain

Schoolchildren are told that the Appalachian Range is relatively old compared with the Rocky Mountains, which is not completely true, but these mountains do have ancient roots, so we will begin at the beginning. Recently, a very detailed summary has been prepared in *The Geology of Virginia* (Read and Eriksson, 2016). For our lay scientific readers, *The Roadside Geology of West Virginia* (Lebold and Wilkinson, 2018) will be rewarding. The geologic record of the border region shared by these two states begins in the Cambrian, about 540 million years ago, and extends to about 300 million years ago, spanning much of the Paleozoic Era. These early rocks are the first to contain an abundant and diverse fossil record, and this makes it possible to reconstruct the history in detail.

The rock formations of the region were initially mapped about 100 years ago but Read and Eriksson have applied recent concepts of Plate Tectonics and Paleoclimatology to their interpretation. As you will see, the border of the Virginias has been quite active tectonically from time to time, and such activity is now known to be typical of passive continental margins. The history of this margin, to judge by the earliest rocks known, begins with a period of continental stretching and rifting, resulting in weakened and thinned continental crust. Such a new "platform margin" would typically subside and accommodate a thick sequence of sedimentary rocks, and importantly it would later be subject to deformation when the tectonic regime switched to the compressive phase. This is mainly because faults were emplaced during rifting, rendering the margin weak. These earliest rocks consist of carbonates (limestone or dolomite.), which are interpreted as deposited in a hot, arid environment when this part of North America was in low latitudes in the southern hemisphere, as verified by paleomagnetic measurements.

The compressive phases in the tectonic regime included three episodes, as outlined by Read and Eriksson. From 460 to 445 million years ago, a collision occurred with an island arc, and this is termed the Taconic Orogeny. At this point a narrow land area resulted along the continental margin, and from this time on, the nascent Appalachians were formed and began shedding sediments to the west, thereby terminating the passive continental margin. Another collision, this time with a microcontinent, occurred from 410 to 360 million years, and this is known as the Acadian Orogeny. Finally, the big one, the continental collision with Gondwanaland, (locally, northwest Africa) occurred from 335 to 260 million years (Scotese & Van der Voo, 1983) and this is known as the Alleghenian Orogeny. Note that during this time of convergence and collision, a mountain range of Himalayan proportions was constructed, and this shed clastic sediments (conglomerates, sandstones, and shales) to the west. Indeed, the advancing mountain range cannibalized these sediments by deforming them and re-eroding them.

The sedimentary stack in the foreland of the rising Appalachians eventually amounted to 19,300 feet thick, as measured in Monroe County, and this is centered in West Virginia and adjacent parts of Ohio (Reger and Price, 1926). This is known as the Appalachian Basin. Paleomagnetic data is included in Read and Eriksson, as well as geologic formation names, rock types, and an interpretation of sea level changes, aridity, and paleotemperature, as the North American continent moved from the southern hemisphere, across the equator, and northern subtropics, to its present position in the warm temperate climate zone. In short, the geologic record may be treated like a giant chart recorder, documenting the changes in sea level, plate motion, and climate zone as they occurred. Altogether, the rock column contains common rocks mentioned in the preceding paragraphs in addition to accessories like coal, iron ore, salt, chert and bentonites (volcanic ash), quite a potpourri to eventually supply minerals for the springs.

Modern Reactivation of The Appalachians

Picking up the story in the middle Jurassic Period, about 150 million years ago, it is clear that the present Atlantic Ocean opened at that time, turning this margin back into an extensional one, again characterized by thinned, subsiding crust which acquired a sedimentary prism, or wedge, thickening toward the east. However, most of the erosional remnants of the Appalachians constitute thick wedges of sediments in deeper parts of both the North Atlantic and the Gulf of Mexico.

Geologists are now turning their attention to recent uplift activity in the Appalachians. These mountains were an important barrier to migration in colonial times, and the question is why have they not been flattened by erosion over the last 260 million years? Studies on the amount of sediment being derived from these mountains suggest that they should be much reduced in height by now, but instead, many areas have elevations of 3 to 4,000 feet and above; and, the river systems are generally quite deeply incised, up to 1,000 feet in the case of the New River Gorge.

Significantly, in 2011 there was an earthquake at Mineral, Virginia of 5.8 magnitude, strong enough to damage both the Washington National Cathedral and the Washington Monument 80 miles northwest. Such events are not unusual along passive margins; they "are thought to reflect reactivation of favorably oriented, generally margin parallel, faults during one or more Wilson cycles by the modern stress field" (Wobin et al., 2012). These researchers go on to say, "This direction is similar to that predicted by models of intraplate stress due to plate-wide forces, including 'ridge push' caused by cooling oceanic lithosphere, mantle flow beneath the continent, and combinations of these and other forces." Could it be that the Atlantic Ocean has begun to close again, and the weakened continental margin is taking up the slack? Recently, it has been shown that the Mineral, VA area is showing signs of reactivation "that ruptured a steeply dipping, northwest-verging reverse fault traversed by the Santa Anna River" (Pazzaglia, et al. 2021, p.595). To the west, in the mountains of northern Greenbrier County, WV, Springer et al. (2015) were able to document stream incision rates of 47 meters per million years based on Uranium-Thorium radioactive dates on uplifted cave stalagmites along Spring Creek. So diverse evidence seems to point to the fact that the Appalachians are again rising at the present time.

Mountains and Springs

One important effect of the presence of mountains on the springs trade is the simple elevation difference from the lowlands, where most of the customers lived and this is because cooler air is found at higher elevations. The south in pre-air conditioner days could be unpleasantly hot in the summer, and diseases like cholera and yellow fever developed in such environments. As has been discussed, plantation owners made a habit of escaping to the spring resorts in the summer for this reason. To find out what the climate differential was in the nineteenth century lowland versus the mountainous south, a simple calculation was performed, and the results are presented in Table 10.1. Here elevations for several lowland and mountain sites are given, together with the calculated July high temperature in Fahrenheit. For this, the *Environmental Lapse Rate* was used, based on the number of 3.56 degrees Fahrenheit per thousand feet. This is an average defined by the International Civil Aviation Organization. To begin with, the temperature at Richmond was selected as a standard because it is at a low elevation of 166 feet on the inner margin of the coastal plain. The July daily high here is 88 degrees at the present time, so we begin by subtracting 1 degree to allow for climate warming in the twentieth century. The figure of 166 feet was subtracted from various spring sites as well as a couple of lowland sites, because Richmond is base line. Hot Springs, VA was added to the local West Virginia sites because it is exceptionally high at 2886 feet. Then the correction factor of 3.56/1000 feet was applied and the July daily high temperature for each location was determined. Note that Red Sulphur was the lowest elevation site among the springs at 1534 feet and it turned out to be 4.9 degrees cooler than Richmond while Hot Springs at 2886' was 77.3 F in July, 9.7 degrees cooler than Richmond, so this would be quite comfortable during the heat of the summer. So, we have quite a range of cooler temperatures for the time traveler to choose from, although the difference would have been only 3.5 degrees if you traveled from Roanoke to Red Sulphur.

Another effect of mountains on springs is gravity which causes precipitation to soak into the rocks, dissolve the more soluble minerals, and transport their dissolved elements to the surface at lower elevations, forming springs. This is known as the artesian flow. As we have seen in the previous sections, these strata are variable in type, representing the changing depositional conditions over nearly three hundred million years. This means that the mineral yield can be quite variable. Also, in mountains may be found large fault zones, which are the result of the earlier collisional deformations. Here we often find hot springs, which tells us that the water is most likely being transported to greater depths in the earth's crust. So, then the thermal expansion of the water is likely driving it back to the surface and providing a heat source to dissolve minerals on the way. In Monroe County, Sweet Springs is hot at 72 degrees, and in nearby Bath County, Virginia, Hot Springs is higher at 100 degrees, whereas the typical spring in this area ranges from 50 to 56 degrees, which is usually described as the "average annual temperature." Hot springs are known from many of the former resort regions and are likely to have initially drawn the attention of prehistoric people.

Table 10.1 Elevation Effects on Temperature (July Maximum)

Name	State	County	Physiographic Province	Elevation	July High
Hot Springs	VA	Bath	Valley & Ridge	2886'	77.3
Old Sweet Springs	WV	Monroe	Valley & Ridge	2030'	80.4
White Sulphur Springs	WV	Greenbrier	Valley & Ridge	1850'	81
Salt Sulphur Springs	WV	Monroe	Appalachian Plateau	1800'	81.2
Blue Sulphur Springs	WV	Greenbrier	Appalachian Plateau	1670'	81.6
Red Sulphur Springs	WV	Monroe	Appalachian Plateau	1534'	82.1
Roanoke City	VA	Roanoke	Great Valley	883'	84.4
Charlottesville City	VA	Albemarle	Inner Piedmont	594'	85.5
Richmond City	VA	Richmond	Inner Coastal Plain	166'	87

Spring Chemistry

The chemical components as well as some physical properties of the local mineral springs are listed in Figure 10.2 and are derived from a massive compilation, *The Springs of West Virginia* (McColloch, 1986). These analyses all date from 1936 so are unlikely to have been altered by spurious modern effects like salt from nearby highways or fertilizer from farmers' fields. The original analyses are listed in "parts per million," but here they have been converted to percentages for each spring. The Discharge and Dissolved Solids, designation are retained in the bottom rows to show that the flow and the concentration of the solids vary by several orders of magnitude between springs. In the original, the order of the chemicals listed is variable by spring, but here it has been made uniform and decreases from top to bottom as a function of the sum of the row, so that the most important ions, generally, are at the top, ranging down to the traces at the bottom, so the various springs may be easily compared, one with another.

At the right side of Table 10.2, a column, Likely Source, is added to the original from information given elsewhere in McColloch (1986, pp.95-99). This is to provide a basis at least for tracing the origin of the spring water to the rock source from which it was derived. It is obvious from this column that evaporites and carbonates occupy the top five rows, and these rock types are ultimately derived from salt ions in the ocean. Evaporites are formed from a range of salt ions that precipitate in coastal lagoons in dry climates and sometimes in desert lakes, while the carbonates, limestone ($CaCO_3$) and dolomite ($CaMg[CO_3]_2$), are "fixed" biologically by sea creatures ranging from corals, clams, algae, including microorganisms. So, carbonates are easily understood as to origin and they do form significant portions of the rock column in this area, of Cambrian to Ordovician age, and of Mississippian age. Carbonates, by definition, are relatively free of clastic sediments like sandstone and mud because they form in dry climates lacking in erosional runoff from the land. The older carbonates are among the oldest in the area and therefore occur where the strata have been pushed up in the Valley and Ridge Province, while the younger carbonates are thinner but broadly distributed in Monroe and Greenbrier Counties and form beautiful farmland.

The evaporites are more problematic as they are not seen in surface exposures in the Monroe County vicinity but have been obtained commercially from wells as close to Red Sulphur Springs as six miles in what is now adjacent Summers County (see Figure 10.3) and also in Greenbrier County (Ziegler, 2019, p.6). In these situations, natural salt springs have been drilled and water pumped down to dissolve a salt layer and then pumped back up and boiled to extract the salt. Also, several residents of western Monroe have reported drilling into salty water on their property. Evidently, there is plenty of salt in the Mississippian age rocks in the vicinity and it must have been dissolved in the surface rocks due to the abundant rainfall or simply escaped detection in this well-vegetated area. Other sources of minerals in spring water include Sandstone (SiO_2) and Iron Ore. Sandstone occurs abundantly in surface rocks, while there are thin but rich iron layers in the local Silurian rocks, a Chalybeate (iron rich) spring is the one labelled White 2 on Table 10.2, and it contains 7% iron.

To make a very long story short, the minerals that we find in the springs today have been assembled during a very long journey, that this portion of the continent has made through tropical and subtropical latitudes during which time the climate has exercised its influence on the ocean chemistry, and therefore changes in the precipitated rock types and ultimately the mineral waters they have yielded.

Table 10.2 Chemistry of Local Springs Compared

	Monroe County Springs				Greenbrier County Springs			Likely Source
	Red	Salt 1	Salt 2	Sweet	Blue	White 1	White 2	
Sulphate (SO_4)	17	59.7	54.5	27.5	52.1	62.2	66.8	Evaporite
Bicarbonate (HCO_3)	53	7.5	13.2	45	12.1	9.3		Carbonate
Calcium (Ca)	10	15.8	15.7	18.8	19.1	19.5	10.1	Carb./Evap.
Sodium (Na) & Potas. (K)	6.4	7.5	6.6	2.3	7.8	1	6.2	Evaporite
Magnesium (Mg)	4.3	4.2	3.9	3.6	3.1	5.8	3	Carbonate
Silica (SiO_2)	3.5	0.9	0.9	1.1	1.5	0.8	6.2	Sandstone
Chloride (Cl)	0.5	3.6	3.6	1.7	3.7	0.8		Evaporite
Iron (Fe)	1.6	0.1			Tr	Tr	7	Iron Ore
Hydrogen Sulphide (H_2S)	3.7	0.9	Tr		0.5	0.6		Org. Shale
Iodide (I)			Tr					
Physical Properties								
Temperature (F)	54	55.4	57.4	72	58	62.5	59	
Discharge (gpm)	0.5	50	50		6	25	0.5	
Dissolved Solids	310	3280	2670	813	1650	2220	88	

> A letter from Mercer County in this State informs us that a rich salt well has recently been discovered in that County, by boring and *tubing* (3 inches diameter) some 600 feet, sufficient to manufacture 300 bushels of salt per day. It is about six miles from the Red Sulphur Springs, and not far from the point where the Louisa Railroad, extended, will touch New River. We are always glad to hear of these developments of old Virginia's treasure.

Figure 10.3 This is one of the only records we have of the mineral salt (Halite) being produced this close to Red Sulphur Springs. (*Richmond Enquirer*, Jan 1, 1850)

Appendices

These diverse tables and articles are peripheral to the main narrative of this book, but are considered too interesting to pass up, so are included for the reader wanting to dig a little deeper into related topics. They were found in out-of-the-way sources like newspapers, courthouse documents, and vintage texts, so would be a challenge to acquire.

Red Sulphur Springs, West Virginia

Appendix One

External Influences on the Economy of the West Virginia Resorts

The Cholera Epidemics had positive influences on the springs because they affected the lowland South and Midwest, and this encouraged the plantation owners to escape to the mountains and patronize the Springs. The Financial Panics had a negative effect simply because the Springs clientele then had limited money for travel. The Civil War was a disaster because hotel space was demanded by the military for lodging and medical facilities, and the ordinary people faced dangerous conditions in venturing forth to travel.

Event	Beginning – End	Duration
Cholera Epidemic	Jun 1832 – Dec 1834	2 yrs., 7 mos.
Financial Panic	May 1837 – Dec 1843	6 yrs., 8 mos.
Cholera Epidemic	Dec 1848 – Aug 1849	9 mos.
Financial Panic	Jun 1857 – Dec 1858	1 yrs., 7 mos.
Civil War	Apr 1861 – May 1865	4 yrs., 2 mos.
Cholera Epidemic	May 1866 – Dec 1866	8 mos.
Financial Panic	Oct 1873 – Mar 1879	5 yrs., 6 mos.
Financial Panic	Jan 1893 – Jun 1894	1 yr., 6 mos.

References:

Aliber, R. Z. and Kindleberger, C.P., 2015, *Manias, Panics, and Crashes: A History of Financial Crises*, p.129

Martindale, Lana, *Highways to Health and Pleasure: The Antebellum Turnpikes and Trade of the Mineral Springs in Greenbrier and Monroe Counties, Virginia*

Peters, S.T., 2005, *Epidemic Cholera: Curse of the Nineteenth Century*

Pyle, G.F., 1969, *The Diffusion of Cholera in the United States in the Nineteenth Century*

Red Sulphur Springs, West Virginia

Appendix Two

Excerpts from Yellow Fever Articles from 1820 to 1830

The source is Newspapers. com, citing only extreme examples reported in Virginia newspapers. The comments on city population are from Google. Cholera is usually stressed as the driver of the Springs trade because it came in distinct cycles, but yellow fever was considered one of the three great killers of the nineteenth century along with cholera and plague (F.M. Snowden, 2020, p.451). With yellow fever, however, slaves were immune because it was an African disease; and ships arriving from the West Indies were the vectors, so the arrival of the disease in North America was very irregular (Snowden, pp.114-5).

Savannah, GA, Aug 1820. "Deaths are from 8 to 10 a day...the town is deserted." (*Alexandria Gazette & Daily Observer*, Sep 4). About ten percent of the population of Savannah died of yellow fever in 1820, in a total population of 14,737.

Natchez, MS, Aug 1823. "We have wretched times in Natchez...eight to ten dying daily, Natchez is nearly deserted" (*Richmond Enquirer*, Sep 26). The population of Natchez in 1830 was just 2,789.

New Orleans, LA, Aug 1824. "The deaths from the 13th to the 19th July were 36, and from the 19th to the 26th, 38...excessive heat has a duration the parallel of which has never been known" (*Richmond Enquirer*, Aug 27).

Mobile, AL, Sep 1825. "The Yellow Fever rages with great violence at Mobile...the inhabitants that were able have fled, not more than 100 remain" (*Richmond Enquirer*, Sep 6). The population of Mobile in 1830 was just 3,194.

New Orleans, Jul 1829. "The Yellow Fever, which has prevailed some time among the shipping, has now completely entered the city, and is making many victims among the unclimated" (*Constitutional Whig*, Richmond, Aug 21).

New Orleans, Sep 1830. "The Yellow Fever was raging there...we would advise to leave the city" (*Daily Richmond Whig*, Sep 23). The population of New Orleans in 1830 was about 51,000 and was the third largest city in the country at the time.

Red Sulphur Springs, West Virginia

Appendix Three

Medicinal Effects of Local Mineral Springs as Summarized in 1835

From Joseph Martin, *New and Comprehensive Gazetteer of Virginia,* (as quoted in P. Reniers, 1941, p.279). This list gives one nineteenth century view of the afflictions that could be treated at the various local mineral springs.

"The **White Sulphur** acts, when taken in doses of two or three glasses at a time, as an alterative, exercising on the system much of the salutary influence, without the evil effects of mercury,--used in larger quantities it becomes actively diuretic and purgative.

The **Salt Sulphur** is more remarkable than The White, for the latter property; but not equal to it in the former.

The **Red Sulphur**, in addition to the qualities which it has in common with the last mentioned springs, is remarkable for its action on the pulse, which it reduces considerably in a short time.

The **Sweet Springs** are of a class of waters called acidulous, and are valuable as a tonic in cases of debility, and in all varieties of dyspepsia which are accompanied by inflammation.

The **Hot Springs** are celebrated for their efficacy in cutaneous, rheumatic, dyspeptic, and liver complaints."

The following are current definitions for the medical terms used above (from *Merriam-Webster and the New Oxford American Dictionary*).

Acidulous: Sharp tasting or sour.

Alterative: A drug used empirically to alter favorably the course of an ailment.

Cutaneous: Of, or relating to, or affecting the skin.

Diuretic: Causing increasing passing of urine.

Dyspepsia: Indigestion.

Purgative: Strongly laxative in effect.

Rheumatic: Marked by inflammation and pain in the joints, muscles or fibrous tissue.

Tonic: A medicinal substance to give a feeling of vigor or well-being.

Red Sulphur Springs, West Virginia

Appendix Four

An 1846 Classification of Mineral Water Types

Here we have some of the best-known examples of mineral springs from Europe and North America (Wm. Burke, 1846, p.44-46), and this will serve to compare Red Sulphur water with other famous examples, near and wide.

"**Natural Waters**, when they are so far impregnated with foreign substances as to have a decided taste and a peculiar operation on the animal economy, are often called Mineral Waters. These are necessarily very diversified in their natures, but they are conveniently arranged for description under four heads, Carbonated, Sulphuretted, Chalybeate, and Saline.

Carbonated Waters are characterized by containing an excess of carbonic acid (H_2CO_3), which gives them a sparkling appearance and the power of reddening litmus paper. These waters frequently contain the carbonates of lime, magnesia, and iron, which are held in solution by the excess of carbonic acid. The waters of Seltzer, Spa, and Pyrmont in Europe, and of Sweet Springs in Virginia, belong to this class.

Sulphuretted Waters contain sulphuretted hydrogen and are distinguished by the peculiar fetid smell of that gas and by their yielding a brown precipitate with salts of lead or silver. Examples of this kind of mineral water are furnished by the waters of Aix La Chapelle and Harrowgate in Europe and those of the White, Red, and Salt Sulphur Springs in Virginia.

Chalybeate Waters * are characterized by a strong inky taste, and by striking a black color with the infusion of galls and a blue one with ferrocyanate of potassa (potassium ferrocyanide ?). The iron is generally in the state of protocarbonate, held in solution by excess of carbonic acid. By standing, the carbonic acid is given off, and the protoxide becomes a hydrated sesquioxide of an ochreous color and is precipitated. The principal chalybeate waters are those of Tunbridge and Brighton in England, and Balston Spa (north of Albany, NY), Bedford (southwest PA), and Brandywine (near Wilmington, DE), in the United States.

Saline Waters are those whose the prominent properties depend on saline impregnation. The salts most usually present are the sulphates, muriates, and soda. The principal saline waters are those of Seidlitz in Bohemia, Cheltenham and Bath in England, and Harrodsburg (central KY) and Saratoga (north of Albany, NY) in the United States."

---

*The Chalybes were an Iron Age people living in northern Asia Minor who specialized in mining iron and were known to the Greeks as a prime source for the material. Hence, their name became synonymous with iron in the classical world (Ziegler, 2014, p.8).

Appendix Five

Red Sulphur Springs District: Interesting History in the Long Ago, 1847-1930

Written by Lewis Preston Campbell and printed in *The Independent Herald*, Hinton, WV, Feb. 12, 1925; originally printed in *The Monroe Watchman* from www.Newspapers.com (Additions in parenthesis, Fred Ziegler). This is the life story of the son of one of the owners of "The Red."

As I am getting old I would like to write a little of my boyhood days, away back in the Forties, from 1847 to the present time. When I was a kid, my Pa (Isaac Henry Campbell, 1808-1861) and Uncle (Thomas S. Campbell, 1806-1860) owned Reed's Bottoms, now called Crump's Bottoms (New River floodplain, below Rich Creek). There were about 800 acres in all---550 acres in bottom land and about 1/4 of it in the woods, that is, of the bottom land. There were lots of big walnut trees, sugar trees, beeches, hickory, poplars, and so on, on the land. There were two large Indian graveyards on the bottom land and in turning the land we would plow up whole Infant skeletons, bones of all kinds, tomahawks, crockery, dishes, arrows and so forth. The land where the camps were was right black and covered with muscle and benawinkle (?) shells and as rich as land could be. My father would turn the land with two yokes of large cattle, and I would drive for him. He used a No.4 Livingston plow.

Corn was our principal crop in those days and would make from 60 to 75 bushels per acre. We would plant about 200 acres every year, and lots of pumpkins, and would feed it out to the hogs, horses, and cattle. We would fatten about 200 head of hogs every year and 100 head of cattle and would drive the hogs to market---to Philadelphia, Baltimore or Richmond and sell them. I do not know how much they got per hundred but I know they would bring back a large roll of old bank notes and pay it out on our land. We would winter about 100 head of cattle and in the spring, turn them out to range in the woods. Pa had a man to look after them and salt them and they would get right fat. Pa kept about ten milch (milk) cows and raised all the calves we could. We kept about 50 shotes (young pigs) thru the winter.

New River was full of fish in those days. If we did not catch a fish on every third or fourth hook we thought it poor fishing. We had all we wanted and nearly always had some on hand.

There were lots of all kinds of field game. Sometimes we would get a fat buck; and lots of coons, opossums, squirrels, wild ducks, and wild turkeys, besides millions of (passenger) pigeons. The pigeons would go off nights to their roosts and we would get sack loads of them. No one knows what ever became of those myriads of pigeons (they became extinct in 1914). They would break great trees down where they roosted and there were many flocks of wild geese passing over every year, ---thousands of blackbirds, and so on.

In those days our schoolhouses were little log huts with one log left out clear across for a window. The floor was a puncheon floor covered with boards. Saplings split open served for our benches. Our teacher would have an old split bottom chair. We got our own wood and made our own fires, and the girls swept the house, and our parents would pay for the schooling.

In 1857 we sold the Bottoms and got thirty-seven thousand, five hundred dollars for the place. There were not many children in those days, like there are now. A few men owned nearly the whole country then. Some of the children would have to go 3 and 4 miles to school.

We did not raise much wheat in those days. It would all fall down. The land was too rich. We would tramp the wheat out with horses or thresh it with a stick and clean it on a sheet. We had biscuits for breakfast every Sunday morning and then they were very dark.

If the fire went out somebody would have to go 3 or 4 miles after fire. There were no matches in those days. Some would have to go 10 or 15 miles for a doctor. There were almost no doctors in the country. Nearly all the men and women that I knew when a boy are dead and gone long ago. My mother could not walk a step for seven years before she died. She was a sufferer from rheumatics of some kind.

We raised flax and our mother would make us boys tow linen (coarse linen) pants. We wore straw hats and if we got a pair of shoes by Christmas, we thought we were doing well. Sometimes we would have to wait until the leather was tanned before we could have our shoes made. Our feet were right tough.

My father never was satisfied after they sold the bottoms. They bought the Red Sulphur Springs and a lot of negroes just a while before the war and lost them all. He and my uncle ran the Red for a while (1856-1861).

The Red Sulphur Springs was a lively place. In the summertime they would have about 300 visitors. Had the best brass band they could get and the very best of living. They would have grand balls at night. Some folks would come for health and some for pleasure, some sick and dying and some dancing.

They had a big store at Red Sulphur. Brother Will was one of the clerks. They hauled all of their goods those days 40 miles. Goods were as cheap then as they are now or cheaper. One dollar would buy as much as three will now.

We boys had a very good time for a while at the Red, but it changed. Our parents died and the Civil War came on. Pa died the 5th of October 1861. Our mother died the 26th of January 1862, and three of us had to go into the war.

Four of us enlisted in the Confederate Army before the war was over and all came out safe except Brother Will. He was killed in battle at New Creek, Maryland, or rather wounded and died nine days afterwards. And the Yankees put Henry in prison and kept him a prisoner a long time. He nearly starved to death and had smallpox and come very near dying of that disease.

We had only one sister, Mary. She married James K. Ballard and had four children, three of who are still living, Stella, Erastus, and Willis. She died July 5, 1888.

When we went into the war, we joined Company A. 17th Regiment of Virginia Calvary. Our Captain's name was James Graybill, under Col. Henderson French. Gen John McCausland was our Brigadier General. Then we had it tough for four years, and when the war was over, and we came home we had hard times for a long time.

I think the nearest I ever got to being killed in time of war was when I and Jack Hatcher were standing behind a large tree loading and shooting time when he was shot through the head and killed. It was a little skirmish fight near Staunton VA. The Yankees were tearing up our railroad, but we made them "git".

After the war everything was torn all to pieces. Money was hard to get. The Union men and the deserters ran the government in those days which made it hard on us "Rebs". They would not let us vote for a long time unless we could take the test oath. The test oath was to swear you never aided the South in any way. But we never took it. In those days the negroes and deserters and Yankees were all that could vote. The good Union men stole two good horses from me, and I could not bring actions unless I could take the test oath. After it got so that we could vote, you would see the Negros gather around the Union men and deserters against the "Rebs" and white men; now it is the Republicans and negroes against the Democrats and white men. Old Monroe for many years after the war was a good Democratic County.

After the war was over the old "Rebs" at Union were hard to keep down. The Yankees had to send troops to Union. There had been several fights there and they were afraid. Some of the old "Rebs" did knock some of them winding. I think a company of Yankee troops stayed at Union over a year after the war before things quieted down.

More hard times came. We never got a cent from our fathers' estate. They sold the Red Sulphur Springs property for Confederate money and our negroes were freed and we lost everything. What little was left our administrator and lawyers go it. And we scattered.

I stayed in old Monroe and got married the 10th of October 1865 (to Isabella Susan Ballard). We soon had a family of children and had it tough until they got big enough to help me. But to think back now, it seems as if that was the best part of my life. There were no railroads, nor coal mines then to bring in the money. What little we got then was by raising tobacco and then it took nearly all to buy the fertilizer; but we managed to keep something to eat and wear. Our nearest railroad depot was 40 miles away at Dublin VA (before 1873).

There were men who did nothing but wagon then; would run 4 and 6-horse teams of the biggest and best horses they could get. Old man Allen Spangler had the best team in the county in those days and wagoned all the time.

Well, I will talk a little about myself. I have had good luck in one way--that is in our children, We have had seven children--five boys and two girls--and they are all living. Never had a death in our family, and I am very thankful. I am writing this for our grandchildren to read when I and their grandma are dead and gone.

There was one thing that happened when we were small that I will never forget. We were working in the field. Pa was plowing, when six great big men rode up and told him they had come to wear him out. They were all brothers. He told them alright if they would come one at a time. He unhitched his team and tied them up and told them he was ready. There was nothing between them but a fence, but they never came over it. He had a knife the blade which was nearly a foot long and if they had crossed that fence, we would have killed the last one of them. He was just in the prime of life and as quick as a cat. They left leaving his fence down, they sneaked off and that was the way they whipped him.

I want to say a few words about my good old father-in-law, Thomas Ballard. He was a remarkable man, good and kind to everybody. He was perfectly deaf but could tell everything you said by the motions of your mouth. He was a strong Confederate in time of the war and a Democrat. He was the strongest man in Monroe County and has been known to knock horses and bulls down with his fist. But he was peaceable and not a maker of trouble. Yet he could have killed a man at one lick.

Appendix Six

A Deed from The Monroe County Courthouse

This document contains an unusual amount of information as it summarizes many earlier deeds and therefore covers the period from 1888 to 1896.

Red Sulphur Springs Water Company, William Noble and Elizabeth Noble, his wife
to Levi P. Morton

(MONROE COUNTY DEED BOOK 33, pp.60-63, November 24th, 1896)

This deed, made this 24th day of November, 1896, between the Red Sulphur Springs Company, a corporation duly organized under the laws of the State of West Virginia, with the right and privilege of holding its principal office and place of business in the City, County and State of New York, William Noble and Elizabeth Noble, his wife, parties of the first part and Levi P. Morton, party of the second part, all of the said City and State of New York.

Witnesseth, that whereas the said Levi P. Morton was on the 13th day of June, 1888, the owner in fee of the Red Sulphur Springs property, situated in Monroe County, West Virginia, embracing twelve hundred to thirteen hundred acres of land, having thereon the well known Red Sulphur Springs, and all the houses, tenements, and fixtures thereon, including the furniture and various other species of personal property. Which property, real and personal, the said Morton and wife, on the date aforesaid, granted and conveyed to Charles H. Lindsley, by their deed of general warranty, recorded in the office of the clerk of the County Court of Monroe County, West Virginia, to which reference is here made for a more full and perfect description of the property aforesaid. But by the said deed the said Morton retained a lien upon the property so conveyed, to secure to him the payment of the sum of $25,000.00, with interest thereon, loaned by him to the said Lindsley.

And whereas, on the same day, June 13th, 1888, the said Charles H. Lindsley and wife by their deed, granted all the property aforesaid, real and personal, to William Morton Grinnell, in trust, to secure to the said Levi P. Morton the sum of $25,000.00, money loaned, and payable July 15th, 1893, with interest thereon. And upon the further trust that the said Lindsley would at his own proper cost, keep insured the buildings and personal property aforesaid against casualties by fire, in the manner in said trust described. That he would also pay all lawful taxes, levies and assessments upon the said property until the debt aforesaid should be fully paid, or caused to be paid. Which trust is also recorded in the office of the Clerk of the County Court of Monroe County, aforesaid in Trust Deed Book no. 1, page 287. And whereas by the execution of the trust deed aforesaid of Lindsley to William Morton Grinnell, the legal title to the property aforesaid was vested in the Said Grinnell as trustee, leaving in the said Lindsley an equity of redemption thereof.

And whereas the said Lindsley and wife, April 18th, 1889, by their deed, also recorded in the Clerk's office of the County Court of Monroe County in Deed Book 28, page 358, conveyed the property to Elizabeth Coates.

And whereas the said Elizabeth Coates widow, by her deed of April 28th, 1889, also recorded in the Clerk's office of the County, Court of Monroe County in Deed Book 29, page 62, conveyed the said property to William Noble.

And whereas the said William Noble and wife, by their deed of February 28th, 1890, also recorded in the Clerk's office of the County, Court of Monroe County in Deed Book 29, page 66, conveyed the said property to the said Red Sulphur Springs Water Company.

And whereas the said Red Sulphur Springs Water Company, possessed of an equity of redemption to the property aforesaid only, by its deed of trust of March 1st, 1890, also recorded in the Clerk's office of the County Court of Monroe County aforesaid in Trust Deed Book No. 2, page 5, did convey the said property in trust to the Holland Trust Company, a corporation duly organized under the laws of the State of New York for the purpose in said deed stated among others, of borrowing money to pay off incumbrances upon the said property, and of carrying on and developing its said property and business, and to pay debts incurred and which will have to be incurred for the necessary uses of the said company, and to accomplish this purpose, the said Red Sulphur Springs Water Company, did, on the__, day of ____. 18__, sign, seal, execute, deliver and issue to the said Holland Trust Company its one hundred (100) bonds, numbered from one to one hundred of the denomination of one thousand dollars each, payable with interest thereon, payable semiannually, as stated in the said deed of trust, to which deed reference is here made for a more specific statement of the covenants and conditions therein contained.

And whereas the said Holland Trust Company, being unable to negotiate a sale of the said bonds, and thereby realize the amount of money necessary for the purposes of the Red Sulphur Springs Water Company, did on the __day of ___, 1896 return to the last named company all of its said one hundred (100) bonds for cancellation or destruction; and at the same time, to wit, on the day and year last aforesaid, did execute and acknowledge for record, and deliver to the said Red Sulphur Springs Water Company, in due form of law its release of the deed of trust aforesaid, thus reinvesting the latter company with the title to the property aforesaid, that was conveyed to it by the said Noble. Reference is here made to the release of the trust deed aforesaid, to which is attached and made part thereof the proceedings, duly authenticated, of a meeting of the Board of Directors of the Holland Trust Company, autoriging (sic) and directing the execution of the release and return of the bonds aforesaid. Which said release, with accompanying papers, it is contemplated, will be recorded simultaneously with this deed.

And whereas the property aforesaid having gone into material dilapidation requiring an outlay of money to restore it to proper condition as a health resort, for the accommodation of guests, and the interest on the trust debt aforesaid, and the taxes on the property having remained unpaid for more than a year, the said Morton instituted his suit in the United States Court for the District of West Virginia, at Clarksburg, to foreclose the trust aforesaid, and the grantor being unable to raise the money to meet these demands and pay the remaining expenses of the property by a sale thereof, in whole or in part, or otherwise, has at its instance, made an amicable arrangement with the said Morton, by which he will accept from the parties of the first part a deed of general warranty for all the property aforesaid, real and personal, specified in the deed aforesaid from himself and wife to Charles H. Lindsley, recorded in the office of the Clerk of the County Court of Monroe County, West Virginia, recorded in Deed Book No. 28, page 154, in full consideration of which the said Morton shall release the lien retained in the deed last named and also secured to him by the trust deed executed by the said Charles H. Lindsley and wife to the said William Morton Grinnell, as trustee.

Now, therefore, this deed further witnesseth that, in consideration of the premises, the Red Sulphur Springs Water Company, William Noble and Elizabeth Noble his wife, parties of the first part, do hereby grant to Levi P. Morton, party of the second part, with covenants of general warranty, all and singular the property aforesaid, real and personal, situated in the County of Monroe, State of West Virginia, and particularly described in the deed executed by the said Morton and wife on June 13, 1888, and recorded in Deed Book No. 28, page 154, above referred to in full consideration whereof, the said Morton has duly executed, acknowledged for record and delivered to the parties of the first part, upon execution of this deed his absolute release of the lien retained by himself in the deed so executed by himself and wife, aforesaid to Charles H. Lindsley, and also further secured by the deed of trust, aforesaid, executed by the said Lindsley and wife to William Morton Grinnell, trustee.

Witness, the following signatures and seals of the said William Noble, and Elizabeth Noble, his wife. And in further testimony whereof the said Red Sulphur Springs Water Company has caused its corporate name to be here unto subscribed by its president, and its corporate seal to be hereunto affixed and attested by its Secretary in pursuance and by virtue of a resolution of its Board of Directors.

William Noble (seal)
Elizabeth Noble (seal)
The Red Sulphur Water Company
By William Noble its President
Attest: Thomas W. Ball Secretary

Appendix Seven

Red Sulphur Owner Wm. Noble Remarries His Wife After Obtaining a Divorce

This is just a funny story about the owner of the Red Sulphur Springs Resort in the years 1889 to 1896. The trip it describes was probably the one during which Mr. Noble became owner. It is included here to inject a little levity into this book—after all the period was the "Gay Nineties." (*The Knoxville Journal,* Tenn., Sun, Dec 22, 1889. Page 4)

William Noble, the millionaire owner of the Grenoble Flats, on fifty-seventh street, New York, has married his wife again. They were divorced last July, and for about two weeks he was a single man. Then the couple had a second wedding trip to Virginia. The fact has been kept very secret, however, and but very few friends of the couple knew that once more their hearts beat as one.

Here is the story of the divorce as told to the New York World when the facts were first published. Mr. Noble is worth a million or more. He is the owner of the handsome Grenoble Flats, on Fifty-seventh street, and various other property in New York City. Besides this, the Atlanta Hotel, at Asbury Park, was until recently one of his possessions. At College Point he owns perhaps the handsomest residence there, while at Red Sulphur Springs, Va. (sic), he holds the title to a fine hotel.

Telling the tale of his domestic woe leading to the divorce which was granted to him in July last, he said that he had discovered his wife's overfondness for a certain musician, Carl Konig, employed by him to amuse the summer residents of his Asbury Park Hotel. Their friendship became the talk of the guests and culminated when she made a pretended attempt to commit suicide by taking a large portion of sugar and water. Afterward, he said, he ordered her to leave his house.

"Why," he exclaimed, with tears in his eyes, "I can never live with this woman again. I would be ashamed to be seen on the streets with her. I could get material for twenty different divorces if I only cared. She can never come near my children again."

Such was Mr. Noble's plaint, and when Lawyer Frank J. Dupignac, who represented his wife, heard the story he ceased to seek a compromise. So, the divorce was duly granted.

But about the middle of August last, Mr. Noble had business which called him south to Red Sulphur Springs, Va. Thither he went. But not alone, for a handsome little woman, dressed in a drab traveling suit, accompanied him. It was his divorced wife, Elizabeth Noble. Numerous telegrams and messages had been sent him during their estrangement, and they soon found their way to his heart. Just where they were united cannot be learned, but it is surmised that the ceremony was performed in Virginia. After a brief sojourn at Red Sulphur the couple returned to New York and Mrs. Noble took up her abode with her brother, Mr. William Weeks. In the meantime, the Noble home at College Point was being put in perfect order, and five weeks ago the old and new mistress in one went there to reside. With her went a retinue of nine servants, a grand stable of high-bred horses and equipages galore.

"In fact," said a former female acquaintance of Mrs. Noble, "from all appearances Mrs. Noble seems benefited pecuniarily from her escapade. She has even more now than before the scandal, and there is little doubt she can have all she wishes for the asking. No, I never hear that he forgave her on condition they should live in the country. They seem to be very fond of each other and may be seen at the theaters frequently on Saturday night."

Mr. Noble is said to have remarked that it cost him $10,000 for his freedom of about two months.

Red Sulphur Springs, West Virginia

Bibliography

Part 1, Published Works

Aliber, R.Z., & C.P. Kindleberger, 2015. *Manias, Panics, and Crashes: A History of Financial Crises,* Palgrave, Macmillan, N.Y. City.

Burke, William, 1842. *The Mineral Springs of Western Virginia.* NY, Wiley & Putnam, Edition 1.

Burke, William, 1846. *The Mineral Springs of Virginia; with Remarks on Their Use, and the Diseases to which They are Applicable,* Wiley and Putnam, NY, (reprint of Sagwan Press).

Burke, William, 1860. *Red Sulphur Springs, Monroe County, Virginia.* Wytheville, VA: D.A. Stelair, Printer.

Cadle, Irma S., 2019. *Jewel of the Meadow: History of the Blue Sulphur Spring.* Grassy Meadows Publishing Co., WV.

Campbell, Robert E.J., 1948. *Random Recollections,* Monroe County Historical Society Collections.

Clark, Thomas N., 1981, *Adam's Ancestors,* A Clark-Harvey Genealogy, Vol I.

Clark, Thomas N. 1999, *Early History of Red Sulphur Springs,* Article in The Monroe Watchman, Oct 28.

Clavin, Tom, 2019. *Wild Bill: The True Story of the American Frontier's First Gunfighter.* St. Martin's Press, NY.

Cohen, Stan, 1981. *Historic Springs of the Virginias,* Pictorial Histories Pub. Co., Charleston, WV.

Cohen, Stan, 1984. *Homestead and Warm Springs Valley, Virginia.* Quarrier Press, Charleston, WV.

Coleman, J. Winston, 1995. *Stage-Coach Days in the Bluegrass.* Univ. Press of Kentucky.

Conte, Robert S., 1998. *The History of the Greenbrier, America's Resort.* Pictorial Histories Pub. Co., Charleston, WV.

Crabtree, Becky H. and Fred Ziegler, 2021. *John Campbell Miller: Builder of Fancy Homes in Rural West Virginia.* 35th Star Publishing Co, Charleston, WV.

Dillion, J.L., Proprietor, ca 1910. Brochure, Monroe County Historical Society, Spring Resorts File.

Dumont, John W., 1987. *Red Sulphur Springs, Background Report.* Privately Pub., Peterstown: WV.

A.Dunlap & Co., *1849-51. Ledger.* Monroe County Historical Society Collections.

Helen S. Ellison, May 1991. *The Red, A Renowned West Virginia Watering Place.* Wonderful West Virginia.

Gillespie, Michael, 2001. *Come Hell or High Water: A Lively History of Steamboating on the Mississippi and Ohio Rivers.* Heritage Press, Stoddard, WI

Gish, Agnes E., 2009, *The Sweet Springs of Western Virginia: A Bittersweet Legacy.* Heritage Books, Westminster, MD.

Gleeson, Dr. J.K.P., 1890-1892. *Letter File of the Manager of Red Sulphur Springs.* Monroe County Historical Society Collections.

Hinton, John, 1827-1829. Red Sulphur Springs Ledger.

Huntt, Henry, 1839. *A Visit to the Red Sulphur Spring of Virginia During the Summer of 1837: with Observations on the Waters.* Dutton & Wentworth Printers, Boston, MA.

Johnson, Viginia, 2019. *Virginia by Stagecoach.* History Press, Charleston, SC.

Jones, R.L., and H.C. Hanson, 1985, *Mineral Licks, Geophagy, and Biochemistry of North American Ungulates.* Iowa State University Press, Ames, IA.

Kessel, Leona, L., 2001, *Monroe County, West Virginia in the Civil War.* Monroe County Historical Society, West Virginia, Informally Published.

Kidd, James R., 1954, *The History of Salt Sulphur Springs.* West Virginia History, a Quarterly Magazine, Vol. XV, No.3.

Kirkwood, James J., 1963, *Waterways to the West.* Eastern National Park & Monument Assoc.

Lebold, J.G., & C. Wilkinson, 2018. *Roadside Geology of West Virginia.* Mountain Press Pub. Co., Montana.

Lederer, R.M., *Colonial American English.* Verbatim, Esex, Connecticut

Leyburn, James C., 1962. *The Scotch-Irish, A Social History.* Univ. North Carolina Press, NC.

Lively, Lester, date unknown., *Bud Dunn Recalls Red Sulphur Turnpike Days.* Hinton Dailey News, Copy in Monroe County Historical Society Files.

Lowry, Terry, 2016. *The Battle of Charleston, and the Kanawha Valley Campaign.* 35th Star Publishing Co. Charleston, WV.

Martindale, Lana, 2017. *Highways to Health and Pleasure: The Antebellum Turnpikes of the Mineral Springs in Greenbrier and Monroe Counties, Virginia.* Monroe County Historical Society, Privately Published.

McColloch, Jane S., 1986. *Springs of West Virginia.* WV Geol. Econ. Surv., Vol. V-6A.

Bibliography

McBride, W. Steven & Kim A. McBride 2012. *Archaeological Investigations of Cook's Fort, 46ME63, Monroe County, WV.* Report Submitted to the Summers County Landmarks Commission.

McKinney, Tim, 2004. *The Civil War in Greenbrier County, West Virginia* Quarrier Press, Charleston, WV.

Miller, James H., 1908. *History of Summers County.* Privately Pub. Hinton, WV.

Monroe Watchman, 1894. *Ideal Summer Homes: Monroe County, West Virginia.* Brochure for 23 Establishments Published by the Watchman.

Morton, Oren F., 1916. *A History of Monroe County, West Virginia.* McClure Co., Staunton, VA.

Motley, Charles, 1973. *Gleanings of Monroe County, West Virginia History.* Commonwealth Press, Radford. VA.

O'Malley, Nancy, 1988, *Taking the Waters: Archaeological Investigations at Five Mineral Springs in Southern West Virginia.* Summers County Historic Landmarks Commission.

Pazzaglia, Frank and 13 others, 2021. *River Terrace Evidence of Tectonic Processes in the Eastern North American Interior, South Anna River, Virginia.* Jour. Geol., Vol. 129.

Perkins, Louise M., 1988. *1850 Monroe County VA (Now WV) Census.* Mountain Press, Signal Mt., TN.

Peters, Stephanie T., 2005. Epidemic: Cholera, Curse of the Nineteenth Century. Benchmark Books, NY

Prolix, Peregrine, 1835. *Letters Descriptive of the Virginia Springs: The Roads Leading thereto, and the Doings Thereat.* H.S. Tanner, Pub. Philadelphia, PA. (Edition Forgotten Books, 2015).

Pyle, G.F., 1969. *The Diffusion of Cholera in the United States in the Nineteenth Century.* Geographical Analysis, Vol.1, p.59-75.

Read, J.F., & K.A. Erikson. 2016, *Paleozoic Sedimentary Successions of the Virginia Valley and Ridge Plateau.* The Geology of Virginia, Virginia Museum of Natural History.

Red Sulphur Springs, 1835-1877, *Hotel Register,* Monroe County Historical Society Collections.

Reger, David B., & Paul H. Price, 1926. *Mercer, Monroe, and Summers Counties.* West Virginia Geological Survey.

Reilly, George J., 2020. *My Father's Livery Stable.* the Carriage Journal Vol. 58, Nov.5.

Reniers, Percival, 1941. *The Springs of Virginia: Life Love and Death at the Waters, 1775-1900.* Chapel Hill, Univ. of North Carolina Press.

Rice, Otis K., 1986. *A History of Greenbrier County.* McClain Printing Co., Parsons, WV.

Schreiber, Harry N., 2011. *Abbot-Downing: Coach and Wagon Makers to the World,* New Hampshire Historical Society, Concord, NH.

Scotese, C.R., & R. Van der Voo, 1983, *Paleomagnetic Dating of Appalachian Folding.* American Geophysical Union, 1983 Spring Annual Meeting, EOS, Vol. 46, Issue 18, p.218.

Shaw, Ronald E., 1990. *Canals for a Nation: the Canal Era in the United States 1790-1860,* Univ. Press: KY.

Shuck, Larry, 1988. *Greenbrier County, Virginia: Early Court Records 1780-1835.* Iberian Pub. Co., Athens, GA.

Shuck, Larry, 1992. *Greenbrier County, Virginia: Deeds and Wills 1777-1833.* Iberian Pub. Co., Athens, GA.

Shumate, H.D., M.N. Banks, L.G. Shumate, & J.W. Banks, 1990. *Cemeteries of Monroe County, West Virginia.* Informally Published, Monroe County Historical Society, Union WV.

Snowden, Frank M., 2019. *Epidemics and Society: From the Black Death to the Present.* Yale University Press, New Haven, CT.

Springer, G.S., H.A. Poston, B. Hardt, & H.D. Rowe, 2015, *Groundwater Lowering and Stream Incision Rates in the Central Appalachian Mountains of West Virginia.* Int. Jour. Speleology, V. 44 (1).

Srinavasan, Bhu, 2017. *A 400-year History of American Capitalism.* Penguin Press: NY.

Supreme Court of Appeals of West Virginia, 1877, *10 W.Va. 662.* Caselaw Project, (Found Online)

Sutphin, G.W., & R.A. Andre, 1991. *Sternwheelers on the Great Kanawha River,* Quarrier Press, Charleston, WV

Trout, W.E., 2002. *A Guide to the Works of the James River & Kanawha Company.* Virginia Canals and Navigation Society.

University of Virginia Library, 2021, *Medicinal Springs of Virginia in the 19th Century.* Exhibits of the Univ. of VA.

Walker, Dr. Thomas, 1750, Reprinted in Summers, Lewis P., 1929. *Annals of Southwest Virginia, 1769-1800.*

White, Sandra, 2013. *Slaves of Monroe County, Virginia.* Informally Published by the Monroe County Historical Society.

Wittenberg, Eric J., 2011. *The Battle of White Sulphur Springs.* History Press, Charleston SC.

Wobin, E., (and 5 others), 2012. *Mineral, Virginia, Earthquake Illustrates Seismicity of a Passive Aggressive Margin.* Geophysical Research Letters, Vol. 39, p.1-7.

Ziegler, Fred. 2014. *Carriages of Monroe County, West Virginia,* Privately Published

Ziegler, Fred, 2019, *The Settlement of the Greater Greenbrier Valley, West Virginia: The People, their Homeplaces, and Their Lives on the Frontier.* 35th Star Publishing Company, WV.

Part Two, Newspapers.com

Included here are over 40 references gleaned from the above website. They are listed by date and the newspaper name and article title are included. The article title is placed in italics, sometimes with a word of explanation if needed.

1825, Apr 22. Charleston Courier, SC, *Botetourt Springs.*

1830, Aug 10. Richmond Enquirer, VA, *Richmond Female Seminary.*

1833, May 22. National Gazette, Philadelphia, PA, *Red Sulphur Springs* (Advertisement).

1833, Jul 30. National Gazette, Philadelphia, PA, *Adam's Latin,* (note, here Latin is misspelled).

1834, Jun 20. Charleston Mercury, SC. *Red Sulphur Springs* (Advertisement).

1836, Aug 8. National Banner & Nashville Whig, TN, *Mail Stage.*

1838, Sep 28. Richmond Enquirer, VA, *President Van Buren* (Visit).

1841, Oct 15. Richmond Enquirer, VA, *Richmond Seminary.*

1842, Jul 8. Richmond Enquirer, VA, *Red Sulphur Springs* (Advertisement).

1843, May 29. Charleston Courier, VA, *Red Sulphur Springs for Sale.*

1844, Jun 29. Daily Madisonian, DC, *Books for Travelers.*

1844, Jul 12. Richmond Enquirer, VA, *To the Editors.*

1845, Oct 31. Richmond Enquirer, VA, *Freight and Passage to Baltimore and Philadelphia.*

1850, Jan 1. Richmond Enquirer, VA , *Letter from Mercer County.*

1855, Jul 31. Richmond Enquirer, VA, *Red Sulphur Springs.*

1856, Jun 25. Charleston Mercury, SC, *Red Sulphur Springs.*

1861, May 2. Richmond Dispatch, VA, *Affairs in Monroe.*

1861, Jun 6. Richmond Dispatch, VA, *Red Sulphur Springs.*

1864, Feb 9. Richmond Dispatch, VA, *A Journey in the Tracks of Averill.*

1865, Sep 30. Shepherdstown Register, WV, *Test Oath.*

1867, Oct 16, Intelligencer, SC. *Robinson's Circus*

1870, Jul 9. Baltimore Sun, MD, *Commissioners Sale of Red Sulphur Springs.*

1871, Jun 28. Richmond Dispatch, VA, *Red Sulphur Springs* (Advertisement).

1871, Jun 28. Richmond Dispatch, VA, *Red Sulphur Rental.*

1873, Nov 13. Daily State Journal, VA. *Capt. Adair Rents Red Sulphur Springs.*

1874, Jan 7. Daily State Journal, VA. *Chesapeake & Ohio Railroad Announcement*

1877, Aug 3. Richmond Dispatch, VA. *Commissioner's Sale of Red Sulphur Springs.*

1877, Aug 14, Alexandria Gazette, VA. *Letter from the Red Sulphur Springs*

1878, Aug 16, Owensboro Examiner, KY. *Letter from West Virginia.*

1878, Sep 26, Richmond Dispatch, VA. *Commissioners Sale of Red Sulphur Spring.*

1881, Jun 18, Baltimore Sun, MD, *Rapid Transit.*

1885, Sep 4, Shepherdstown Register, WV. *Visit of L.P. Morton to Red Sulphur Springs.*

1885, Nov 30. Wheeling Daily Register, WV/ *General News.*

1887, Feb 18, Shepherdstown Register, WV. *Capt. Adair* (Death Note).

1904, Jan 9, Hinton Daily News. *Monroe Railroad.*

1909, Jan 23, Clarksburg Daily News, WV. *Morton Gives Red Sulphur Springs to the State.*

1909, Jan 25, Clarksburg Daily Telegram, WV. *Col. Ben Wilson.*

1917, Jun 17, Louisville Courier Journal, VA. *The Red Sulphur Springs Hotel Will Open July 1.*

1917, Jul 9, Hinton Daily News, WV. *Many Hinton People at Red Sulphur Springs.*

1918, Nov 9, Hinton Daily News, WV. *Red Sulphur May Fall to Government.*

1923, Sep 5, Hinton Daily News, WV, *Lilly Confident of U.S. Prison.*

1925, Feb 12, Hinton Independent Herald, WV, *Interesting History in The Long Ago,* (by L.P. Campbell).

1932, Aug 15, Hinton Daily News. *A Hotel At Red Sulphur Was Burned.*

Index

Abbott and Downing 33, 34
Adair, Ann (Harvey) 63
Adair, William 60, 61, 63
Anderson, Henry 51
Argroves, M.M. 54
Ashworth, John 51
Austin, Wm. W. 17
Averell [Averill], William W. 56
Baber, Hanton 51
Baber, Powhatan 51
Baldwin, A.F.M. 54
Ball, Thomas W. 107
Ballard, Erastus 102
Ballard, James K. 102
Ballard, Mary (Campbell) 102
Ballard, Stella 102
Ballard, Thomas 103
Ballard, Willis 102
Barton, Willson 51
Beirne, Andrew 14, 22, 30, 43, 44, 45
Beirne, Eleanor Grey (Keenan) 43
Beirne, George 43
Beirne, Margaret Melinda (Caperton) 43
Beirne, Oliver 43, 44, 45, 51, 56
Belcher, H.C. 18
Benson, Ervan 9
Blue, Hubert
Blue Sulphur Springs 1, 7, 9, 55, 88, 89
Botetort Springs 20
Bowyer, Michael 9
Brown, William 51
Buckingham, James Silk 26
Bullitt, Thomas 9
Burke, Christianna 21, 22
Burke, Thomas J. 21, 51, 52
Burke, William 1, 2, 4, 5, 13, 14, 15, 16, 21, 22, 23, 25, 26, 30, 43, 44, 45, 52
Burkett, Peter T. 54
Burnsides, John 43
Burrill, George 17
Cabell, John 6, 9
Callaway, Christopher 51
Callaway, Garner 51
Callaway, Joshua 51

Camp, Wm. 51
Campbell, C.W. 2
Campbell, Charles W. 81, 84
Campbell, Elizabeth 45
Campbell, Isaac H. 44, 45, 60, 63, 101
Campbell, Isabella Susan (Ballard) 103
Campbell, Lewis M. 84
Campbell, Lewis P. 45, 101-103
Campbell, Mary K. (Johnson) 63
Campbell, Nancy A. (Vass) 45
Campbell, Robert D. 60, 61, 63
Campbell, Samuel 45
Campbell, Thomas S. 44, 45, 46, 51, 60, 63, 101
Campbell, Jr., William 51, 102
Campbell, Sr., William 51
Caperton, Capt. Hugh 6
Caperton, Hugh and Rhoda 6
Carvile, John W. 18
Ceebrook, W.B. 18
Clark, Thomas N. 11
Coates, Elizabeth 70, 105
Cohen, Stan 81, 83, 85
Coleman, Thos. B. 18
Cooke, George Esten 2, 22, 24, 25
Coon, Wm. R. 54
Cooper, G. 18
Costa, Jim 2, 16
Cottle, Madison 51
Cowles, G.H. 45
Crosier, J.H. 67
Cummins, John 51
Cutler, Mons. 65
David, Isaac 54
Dawson, William M.O. 79
Day, Hiram 65
Dillard, P.H. 84
Dillion, J.L. 79
Doss, Jesse 54
Dumont, John W. 4
Dunlap & Co. Store 4, 47, 48, 63
Dunlap, Addison 30, 44, 45, 47, 48, 51, 60, 61
Dunlap, Alexander 30, 44, 45, 47, 51, 60, 63
Dunlap, Benjamin M. 48
Dunlap, Elizabeth Clara (Petrie) 45
Dunlap, Francis Catherine (McElhenny) 45
Dunlap, James A. 22, 30, 44, 45
Dunlap, Jane Alexander 45

Dunlap, Mary Ann 44, 45
Dunn, Charles A. "Bud" 75
Dunn, Madison 51
Dupignac, Frank J. 109
Eads, Joshua 51
Echols, John (Echols' Brigade) 56
Edgar, Thomas and Ann 6
Elkins, Wm. 54
Ellison, Isaac J. 51
Ellison, Helen 76
Fantain, T. 18
Finch, H.G. 54
Floyd, John B. (Floyd's Brigade) 55, 56
Fowler, Mrs. 52
Fowler, Thomas 51
Fox, Haywood 54
Francis, John W. 51
French, Henderson 102
Ganss, Arch 51
Gartin, Goodall 51
Gentry, John 54
Gestaves, Deep 18
Gist, John 17
Gleeson, J.K.P. 4, 72, 73, 74, 75, 79
Goodall, Tiny 51
Graham, H. 18
Graybill, James 102
Grey [Gray] Sulphur Springs 1, 9, 16, 55, 56
Grinnell, William Morton 70, 105, 106, 107
Gwinn, Sam'l 51
Hampton, Rob. 17
Hansbarger, E.C. 2
Hansbarger, J.E. 81, 84
Harrell, S.W. 81, 84
Harrison, Benjamin 69, 71
Harrison, H.T. 17
Harvey, James 1, 2, 5, 9, 11, 13, 14, 16, 63
Harvey, John 1, 5, 11, 14
Harvey, John and Margaret 6
Harvey, Nancy (Snidow) 14
Harvey, Nicholas 1, 5, 6, 9, 10, 11, 13, 14, 75
Harvey, Sarah Ann 6, 14
Hatcher, Jack 102
Havesham, Mrs. 18
Haynes, Alexander 44, 51, 60, 63
Haynes, William 48, 51
Herbert, J.B. 17

Hereford, Frank 70
Heth, Henry 54
Hinton, John 4, 13, 16
Hodge, Lelia 67
Hooper, Thos. 17
Hot Springs 1, 7, 9, 20, 87, 88
Houston, A.C. 67
Hughart, Dan'l 54
Humphreys, S.F. 75
Huntt, Henry 4, 9
Hurlbut, Prof. 65
Hutchinson, John M. 51
Jefferson, Thomas 30
Jennings, Harry 65
Johnson, L.P. 67
Johnston, Albert Sydney 81
Kirkpatrick, Thomas and Jenny 6
Koch, Robert 2, 75, 81
Konig, Carl 109
Krenshaw, Dr. 56
Larew, John M. 51
Larew, Mrs. 51
Lee, Robert E. 56
Legare, John D. 9, 14, 16
Lewis, Alfred 17
Lewis, John B. 9, 30
Lewis, William 9
Lewis, Zebedee 51
Lincoln, Abraham 59
Lindsley, Charles H. 70, 105, 106, 107
Lindsley, Sylvia A. 70
Lively, Levi 51
Loring, William W. 55
Lynch, C.E. 67
Madison, John 18
Malone, Henry 17
Mathew's Trading Post 48
Marke, Newton 18
Maxwell, Solomon D. 54
McCartney, James H. 51
McCausland, John 56, 102
McCormick, John 17
McDonald, Dr. 67
McKim, John 17
Meadows, Christopher 54
Miller, John 51
Miller, Samuel 51

Mitchell, L. 17
Molloy, Rev. J.D. 61
Monroe, James M. 51
Montgomery, Fred 18
Moomaw, H.M. 84
Morris, Hugh R. 18
Morton, Anna L. 70
Morton, Frank 69
Morton, Levi P. 1, 60, 63, 64, 69, 70, 71, 75, 77, 79, 81, 82, 91, 105, 106
Morton, Oren F. 4, 64
Motley, Charles 4
Myddleton, W.J. 18
Nicholson, Carlina 17
Nicholson, James M. 54
Nisornon, Joseph 51
Noble, Elizabeth 70, 84, 105, 106, 107, 109
Noble, William 69, 70, 84, 105, 106, 107, 109
O'Malley, Nancy 4
Pack, Bartet 48
Palmer, R.D. 18
Patton, James F. 67
Payne, Phillip 17
Pearce, Miss R. 73
Pence, David 51
Phillips, Samuel 51
Phillips, William B. 30
Phipps, George W. 54
Poe, Edgar Allan 48
Prentice, James 51
Preston, Rev. Mr. 26
Prolix, Peregrine 26, 28, 29
Raffner, David S. 51
Richie, Josiah 54
Rippetoe, Lafayette 54
Roach, Isaac 51
Robinson, Conway 14, 22
Robinson's South-Western Circus 65, 66
Rockbridge Alum Springs 1
Rorer, P.H. 81, 84
Rose, John 17
Royall, Jone 18
Ryan, Wm. 54
Salt Sulphur Springs 1, 7, 9, 20, 25, 28, 55, 56, 57, 65, 76, 88, 89
Saunders, Holeman 51
Scrugs, J.P. 18
Seal, James W. 51
Shanklin, Absolom 51
Shanklin, Davidson 51
Shanklin, Richard V. 44, 51, 60, 63
Shanklin, Mary (Pack) 63
Shannon, Newson 54
Slaughter, Martin 17
Smith, Green T. 54
Smith, Zachariah 54
Spangler, Allen 103
Spencer, Wm. W. 51
Strickland, William 13
Sultana 37
Sutphin, David 54
Swinney, Vincent 51
Sweet Springs 1, 9, 20, 30, 43, 53, 55, 56, 57, 65, 76, 87, 88, 89
Sydnor, Abram 18
Tardy, Paul J. 17
Taylor, Henry 51
Taylor, Moses 51
Taylor, Samuel 54
Terrel, Wm. B. 54
Thrasher, Robert 51
Tickle, Solomon D. 54
Tines, H. 17, 18
Twain, Mark 33
Umbarger, Andrew 54
Van Buren, Martin 22, 26
Vass, Boswell 51
Vass, James 51
Vass, Wm. 51
Walker, Freeman 17
Walker, Thomas 7, 17
Walls, Moses P. 54
Walls, William M. 54
Warm Springs 1, 7, 9, 20, 26, 28
Warrenburg, Wm. 51
Washington, George 38, 65
Watson, Ben B. 17
Watson, Rich P. 17
Way, Mrs. 51
Weeks, William 109
Wharton, Gabriel C. (Wharton's Brigade) 56
White, W.C. 54
White Sulphur Springs 1, 9, 20, 25, 28, 55, 56, 57, 65, 88, 89
Williams, John S. 55

Wilson, Allen 18
Wilson, Benjamin 60, 69
Wilson, David 18
Wilson, Joseph 17
Winstead, Alex 18
Wise, Henry A. (Wise's Brigade) 56
Wooden, E.W. 51
Workman, David 54
Young, Elisha 54
Young, Robert 17

About the Author

Alfred "Fred" Ziegler retired in 2003 from teaching and researching Historical Geology and Paleogeography after 37 years at the University of Chicago. He sponsored The Paleogeographic Atlas Project which produced many scientific studies on reconstructing the geography and biogeography of the earth for various stages in its long history. Then he moved to West Virginia where he and his wife Barbara bought "Cooks Old Mill," established in the 1770's by Valentine Cook in what would later become Greenville. Fred found himself in the middle of some very interesting local history and changed gears from millions to hundreds of years and began writing books: *The Carriages of Monroe*, *The Settlement of the Greater Greenbrier Valley*, and *John Campbell Miller, Builder of Fancy Homes in Rural West Virginia*. The present book on Red Sulphur Springs describes one of four resorts which made Monroe County the center of tourism in the nineteenth century, although The Red has been gone and largely forgotten for the last hundred years.

Fred has served as president of the Monroe County Historical Society and spearheaded the building of the Carriage House Museum in Union. The Museum now has eight full-size horse-drawn vehicles, including an Omnibus which at one time conveyed visitors to resort spas at Sweet Springs and Chalybeate Springs. Fred also has served as the chairman of the local Landmarks Commission and in this connection helped to sponsor the Archaeological Investigation of Cooks Fort, another colonial construct of Valentine Cook, and this study was carried out by Steven and Kim McBride recently. Finally, the West Virginia Department of Arts, Culture and History has recently presented Fred a West Virginia History Hero certificate "for outstanding work and significant contributions to preservation and promotion of West Virginia History."

35th Star Publishing
Charleston, West Virginia
www.35thstar.com

www.ingramcontent.com/pod-product-compliance
Lightning Source LLC
LaVergne TN
LVHW070532070526
838199LV00075B/6760